THE DARK YEARS?

PHILOSOPHY, POLITICS, AND THE PROBLEM OF PREDICTIONS

JACOB L. GOODSON

CASCADE *Books* · Eugene, Oregon

THE DARK YEARS?
Philosophy, Politics, and the Problem of Predictions

Cascade Books
An Imprint of Wipf and Stock Publishers
199 W. 8th Ave., Suite 3
Eugene, OR 97401

www.wipfandstock.com

PAPERBACK ISBN: 978-1-5326-5388-9
HARDCOVER ISBN: 978-1-5326-5389-6
EBOOK ISBN: 978-1-5326-5390-2

Cataloguing-in-Publication data:

Names: Goodson, Jacob L., author.

Title: The dark years? : philosophy, politics, and the problem of predictions / Jacob L. Goodson.

Description: Eugene, OR: Cascade Books, 2020 | Includes bibliographical references and index(es).

Identifiers: ISBN 978-1-5326-5388-9 (paperback) | ISBN 978-1-5326-5389-6 (hardcover) | ISBN 978-1-5326-5390-2 (ebook)

Subjects: LCSH: Rorty Richard. | Philosophy and religion. | Pragmatism.

Classification: B945.R524 .G66 2020 (paperback) | B945.R524 .G66 (ebook)

Manufactured in the U.S.A.   08/02/20

THE DARK YEARS?

Dedicated to Sophia Grace and Seraphina Rose:
For your futures, for your sake, for your well-being . . .
Rorty predicts darkness during the best years of your lives.
My *hope* for you is that he is more wrong than right
and the arguments of this book become superfluous.

Contents

Acknowledgments

On occasion, throughout the book, I have mentioned how this was an emotionally difficult book to write. Of course, writing any book comes with emotional difficulty. This book struck me especially hard because my previous books allowed for a healthy escape from the daily noise and stream of news media, social media, etc. Writing this book, however, seemed to obligate me to pay closer attention to these streams. For instance, I actually kept a journal record of when "mass shootings" were reported and took notes in relation to Stanford's standards about mass shootings. My youngest daughter took notice of this, which understandably increased the amount of fear she feels about guns and gun violence. On some days, I feel (I say "feel" instead of "think") that her fear of gun violence proves that we are indeed in a period of "dark years" of American life; children should not have to live in fear of their own fellow citizens. I dedicate this book—with the *hope* that Rorty's predictions are more wrong than right—to both of my daughters, Sophia Grace and Seraphina Rose; the next thirty years should be a time of *flourishing*, and nothing less, for both of you!

Support for the book came from several different sources, both individual and institutional: the Kirk Fund (the Philosophy and Religion endowment for research at Southwestern College), Larry and Linda Hahn (Winfield, Kansas), Rev. Phil Kuehnert (Williamsburg, Virginia), David and Shannon Lewis (Edmond, Oklahoma), Rev. Alan Lindal (Wichita, Kansas), Claire and Gene Partlow (Williamsburg, Virginia), and the Scriptural Reasoning Network. I remain grateful to all of them.

Context matters for writing. While most of this manuscript was written from my home office, I benefit a great deal from having a few comfortable and reliable places to write: Aeroplanes Brewery in Wichita, Kansas; College Hill Coffee in Winfield, Kansas; The Patriarch in Edmond, Oklahoma; Steamy Joe's in Arkansas City, Kansas; and Wheat State Winery in Winfield, Kansas.

Scholars who read parts of the manuscript and offered comments and suggestions along the way include: Dr. Andrew Cutrofello (Professor of Philosophy, Loyola University Chicago), Dr. Stanley Hauerwas (Emeritus Professor of Theological Ethics at Duke Divinity School and Emeritus Professor of Law at Duke University), Dr. Sam Martin (Professor of Communication and Rhetoric, Southern Methodist University), Dr. David Nichols (Emeritus Professor of History and Economics at Southwestern College), Dr. David O'Hara (Professor of Philosophy and Classics, Augustana University), Dr. Justin Olmstead (Associate Professor of History, University of Central Oklahoma), Dr. Dianne Rothleder (Lecturer, Loyola University Chicago), and Dr. Brad Elliott Stone (Professor of Philosophy, Loyola Marymount University). I feel so much gratitude toward those who read my works-in-progress and contribute to improving the final product. I met with Dr. Nichols and Dr. Olmstead an average of once per week to talk through the manuscript, and they discussed their writing projects with me as well; I benefit greatly from those weekly meetings. Some current and former students read portions of the manuscript as part of class requirements, and their feedback improved particular arguments: Melissa Connell, Nick Detter, Drake Foster, Meghan Kindred, Quinlan Stein, and Emily Sutton. I am blessed by being surrounded by such smart students who are careful readers!

Certain chapters were first given as lectures or presentations: chapter 3 at a conference on Christianity and Literature in Shawnee, OK (September 2018); chapter 5 at a conference on the history of rhetoric in Austin, TX (February 2019); and a portion of the conclusion was given as the Hall of Fame Lecture at Southwestern College in Winfield, KS (April 2018). Rowman & Littlefield allowed me to republish part of chapter 5, originally published as chapter 15 in *American Philosophers Read Scripture*. Part of chapter 7 was previously published in the *Journal of Scriptural Reasoning*; permission has been granted by the general editor. Cascade Books granted permission for me to quote extensively from Stanley Hauerwas's *Minding the Web: Making Theological Connections*.

Of course, I owe much of my writing career thus far to Dr. Charlie Collier—who believes in me more than I believe in myself. He initially conceived the idea of a whole book on Rorty's predictions, and I am glad that he did. Charlie is an ideal editor for a scholar. Finally, I must mention that Dr. Donald Wester initially introduced me to Richard Rorty's writings. Because of Dr. Wester, I started seriously reading Rorty's work on Christmas day in 1999—which means that I have spent twenty years wrestling with Rorty's thought (this length of time occurred to me only while wrapping up the manuscript). Dr. Wester died on May 31st, 2019—before the manuscript was completed. I deeply miss him.

Abbreviations

AOC   Richard Rorty, *Achieving Our Country: Leftist Thought in Twentieth-Century America*

CIS   Richard Rorty, *Contingency, Irony, and Solidarity*

FNT   James Baldwin, *The Fire Next Time*

HDB   Joseph Richard Winters, *Hope Draped in Black: Race, Melancholy, and the Agony of Progress*

OD   Robert Talisse, *Overdoing Democracy: Why We Must Put Politics in Its Place*

PBL   Richard Rorty, "Postmodernist Bourgeois Liberalism"

PC   Martha Nussbaum, "Patriotism and Cosmpolitanism"

PCRR   Robert Talisse, "A Pragmatist Critique of Richard Rorty's Hopeless Politics"

PS   John McCumber, *The Philosophy Scare: The Politics of Reason in the Early Cold War*

PRP   Richard Rorty, "Pragmatism as Romantic Polytheism"

PSH   Richard Rorty, *Philosophy and Social Hope*

RH   Akiba J. Lerner, *Redemptive Hope: From the Age of Enlightenment to the Age of Obama*

RR   Neil Gross, *Richard Rorty: The Making of an American Philosopher*

RE   Richard Rorty, "Redemption from Egotism"

SM   Jacob L. Goodson, *Strength of Mind: Courage, Hope, Freedom, Knowledge*

SS   Ronald A. Kuipers, *Solidarity and the Stranger: Themes in the Social Philosophy of Richard Rorty*

TD   John McCumber, *Time in a Ditch: American Philosophy and the McCarthy Era*

TWO   Richard Rorty, "Trotsky and the Wild Orchids"

WF   Dianne Rothleder, *The Work of Friendship: Rorty, His Critics, and the Project of Solidarity*

Introduction

Predictions Run in the Family

IN THE YEAR 1936, the Great Depression loomed over American politics and society. In the same year, a journalist—a critic of communism and defender of socialism—published a book entitled *Where Life Is Better: An Unsentimental American Journey.*[1] *Where Life Is Better* explores "the nation's 'temperament,'" and it addresses the following questions: "What is going to happen? Do we have to copy Europe? What is American? What can we cherish and nourish ourselves?"[2] In order to address these questions with journalistic integrity, the author drove from New York to California talking to American citizens in Chicago and Detroit, Minnesota and Wisconsin, and Hollywood and San Francisco. About citizens in San Francisco, for instance, the author criticized flirtation with communism. The author thought there must be better ways out of the Great Depression than what the American Communist Party offered America. However, one of the judgments of the author is that indeed "life is better" in California; the signature chapter of the book bears a similar title to the cover: "California, Where Life Is Better."[3] The author was in California for so long that his abandoned spouse wrote requesting that he return home and spend time with their son. Knowing the title of the forthcoming book and wanting his father back home, their five-year-old son scribbled in a letter: "New York: Where Life Is Better."[4]

---

1. For the sake of suspense, I break conventional citation standards and cite only the titles of these books—*Where Life Is Better* and *McCarthy and the Communists*—so as to conceal the identity of the author. I also rely on a secondary source—Neil Gross's *RR*—to fill in some of the details about this author and these two books.

2. Gross, *RR*, 76.

3. See *Where Life Is Better*, 269–331.

4. See Gross, *RR*, 88.

Where Life Is Better makes strong predictions: the Great Depression would lead the United States of America to dictatorial rule, fascism, and participation in another world war. The author alerts readers to these predictions in the "Introduction": "The present is tragic enough; the years ahead will be even more tragic in all probability."[5] The author grounded these predictions on the weakness of democratic institutions: "We have . . . an established system . . . in the operation of which one class of the population has been encouraged . . . to exploit the other classes."[6] This exploitation makes America look like Europe prior to the First World War, and the author uses this observation to predict that America will find itself participating in another world war: "It struck me that the democratic dogma would probably crack at the periphery before it cracks at the center; that in Wisconsin and Minnesota the necessary class fission was more or less imminent"; before "that happens," however, "the center . . . will . . . cast the dice for martial suicide in the next [world] war."[7] Either America would see the likes of a communist revolution (in the Midwest of all places!) or it would prevent such a revolution from happening by entering into war. The author predicts that the latter will come true. Bolstering this prediction, the author concludes *Where Life Is Better* with the sobering judgment: "[I]t will be easy to recruit the unemployed for . . . war."[8]

Alongside the exploitation of the working classes, which meant the weakness of democratic institutions, the author also worried about the severe economic vulnerabilities caused by the Great Depression—which led to tendencies toward American nationalism and anti-Semitism found in a rising populism.[9] The author equated the decline of capitalism with fascism: "[T]he logic of capitalism in its present period of decline . . . is the logic of fascism."[10] The more detailed yet precise version of this judgment is: "Our domestic situation is that of a progressively deteriorating social and economic anarchy, with a definite drift toward fascism."[11] A reader, who read a

---

5. *Where Life Is Better*, 50.

6. *Where Life Is Better*, 169.

7. *Where Life Is Better*, 170.

8. *Where Life Is Better*, 383.

9. "This structural weakness, when combined with economic vulnerability and what [the author] saw as rural populism's tendency toward nationalism and anti-Semitism, rendered the likelihood of an American turn to fascism high" (Gross, *RR*, 50).

10. *Where Life Is Better*, 343.

11. *Where Life Is Better*, 380.

draft of *Where Life Is Better* prior to its publication, alarmingly agreed with the author's prediction about America becoming a fascist nation. In the published version of *Where Life Is Better*, the author included the reader's agreement as a footnote: "At the present state of mind of our population, I am afraid the granting of such power could mean nothing but a step toward fascism."[12] This comment leads the author to offer a definition of fascism not found in the body of the text: "Fascism . . . combines the maximum of power with the maximum of irresponsibility, and the domestic and international chaos which it ultimately precipitates is far more difficult to liquidate than the confusions of the quasi-democratic states." In addition to leading the US to another world war, the author predicts that the Great Depression will lead to electing a dictator who maximizes power but ignores the responsibility the government has to its citizens and to other countries. The result will be "chaos," "confusion," and class inequality.[13]

Despite the suggested promise of the title, *Where Life Is Better* ends in a tone of hopelessness and pessimism. The author attempts a different ending but does not succeed. The optimism of "Life can be made better in America. Indeed, America can be made quite magnificent," is followed by "But not by those who dream dead dreams, who plead exemption from struggle on one ground or another, who cry for peace but will not pay its price."[14] Only one of the concrete predictions turned out to be accurate: America entered into a world war after the Great Depression (WWII). America neither experienced fascism nor saw a dictator rise to power in the timeframe constructed and imagined by the author.

Twenty-eight years later, the same author—this time with an additional coauthor—published a journalistic analysis of Senator Joseph McCarthy and McCarthyism within American politics. What is the link between the books *Where Life Is Better* and *McCarthy and the Communists*? The connection concerns the impact of populism nurtured in the Midwestern part of the United States. In *McCarthy and the Communists*, the authors claim that "Midwestern populism" allowed for the "totalitarian" tactics known as McCarthyism:

> Senator McCarthy is not a unique phenomenon in American political history. He stems from the frontier tradition rooted in the Midwest. The frontiersmen . . . carved out their own fortunes and produced a new image of individualism in America. The hero

12. *Where Life Is Better*, 170.

13. *Where Life Is Better*, 170.

14. *Where Life Is Better*, 383.

of this image was independent, self-reliant, virile, strong, simple, and direct. This rough-and-ready customer had little time for education, considered culture suspiciously effeminate, and was ignorant or contemptuous of Old World refinement and Eastern gentility. The politics that emerged in the Midwest, populist and conservative alike, was closely related to this image of individualism . . . . In this atmosphere, simple, unsophisticated, and uncomplicated panaceas could be put forward as solutions for large, complex problems. The region became a breeding ground for demagogues and demagoguery.[15]

With this paragraph, we might think that the authors conclude that the earlier predictions made in *Where Life Is Better* have been fulfilled because of Senator McCarthy and McCarthyism. The authors of *McCarthy and the Communists*, however, disavow any and every claim pertaining to McCarthyism as a form of fascism—"people have been careless about applying the word 'fascist' to McCarthy"—implying that McCarthyism did not fulfill predictions made, twenty-eight years earlier, in *Where Life Is Better*.[16] The author did not coauthor *McCarthy and the Communists* in order to boast about the previous predictions found in *Where Life Is Better* but, rather, to make new predictions and to offer suggestions for preventing these predictions from coming true.

If the US continues to be defined and determined by "Midwestern populism," the authors predict that McCarthyism will lead to a version of totalitarianism. They describe totalitarianism in the following terms: "Totalitarianism is a unique product of the twentieth century which demonstrates that everything is indeed possible, which plumbs the depths of human depravity." They continue by claiming that totalitarianism results from "the process of atomization of society which in our time has made it possible to translate individual men into the . . . unknown phenomenon of mass-man." In addition to being a "political phenomenon," totalitarianism "is a spiritual movement, possessing comprehensive ideological scope and global political aspirations"—which "demands of its adherents unquestioning, inflexible discipline and an all-embracing loyalty."[17] They complete their description of totalitarianism with words that deeply matter for their prediction:

15. *McCarthy and the Communists*, 110.
16. See *McCarthy and the Communists*, 113.
17. *McCarthy and the Communists*, 114.

Totalitarianism depends both on the ability of the leader to harness political power and on the political susceptibility of the followers. No one can judge precisely whether any man is a potential totalitarian leader unless it is known that the society within which he moves has political characteristics that would make it prone to submit to totalitarianism.[18]

The authors claim here that predicting totalitarianism ought to be considered a difficult, serious task. They spend the remainder of their chapter thinking through the question "Is McCarthy a totalitarian?" They certainly think that McCarthy, himself, seeks totalitarian power.[19] Because the answer depends on "the political susceptibility of the followers," however, their own answer must remain vague. In the combination of McCarthy's desire for power and the tendencies of "Midwestern populism," they see the "potential" for totalitarianism in the US.[20] They predict that McCarthyism will lead either to totalitarianism or—if not to that extreme—to a lengthy period of anti-education and anti-intellectualism in American politics and society.[21]

Before I reveal the author of these predictions, I consider the author's predictions concerning the results of McCarthyism. The US did not fall to totalitarianism, but did it find itself in a lengthy period of anti-education and anti-intellectualism? One philosopher thinks so. A professor at Northwestern University in Evanston, Illinois, John McCumber, has published detailed analyses and research on how McCarthyism impacted colleges and universities.[22] In particular, McCumber finds that McCarthyism muzzled the mouths of philosophy professors throughout the US for a very lengthy period—perhaps up until the 2000s. McCumber claims that McCarthyism led to the tendency within philosophy to no longer think of philosophy as a discipline relevant to society but one that only analyzed language and provided conceptual foundations for the natural sciences.[23] What we refer

18. *McCarthy and the Communists*, 114.

19. "Senator McCarthy as a power-seeking demagogue is clearly a force to be contended with" (*McCarthy and the Communists*, 110).

20. Their main distinction in the chapter, "Is Senator McCarthy a Totalitarian?" is that between "actual and potential" totalitarianism (see *McCarthy and the Communists*, 109–24).

21. See *McCarthy and the Communists*, 125–47.

22. I am grateful to Brad Elliott Stone for directing my attention toward McCumber's research.

23. See McCumber, *TD*, 33–58.

to as "Analytic Philosophy," according to McCumber's research, ought to be considered the product of McCarthyism. Now, "Analytic Philosophy" existed prior to Joseph McCarthy and McCarthyism—in the work of A. J. Ayers, Gottlob Frege, Bertrand Russell, and others—but McCumber's insight is that it ruled itself as the only legitimate form of philosophy within the US *because of McCarthyism*.[24] Doing "Analytic Philosophy" shields philosophers from being accused of impacting politics, policy, and society. In other words, it prevents philosophers from being charged with "corrupting the youth"—the famous charge against Socrates.[25] Although "Analytic Philosophy" remains a very high educational and intense intellectual school of thought, can it be considered "anti-education" and "anti-intellectual" in the sense of disallowing and failing to promote learning and rationality for the sake of making judgments about and against politics and society? McCumber thinks so. "Analytic Philosophy" refuses judgments against politics and society (or, at least, holds them in suspicion), and—*very much unlike Socrates*—the way that "Analytic Philosophy" works is that it makes itself a tool for the defense of the status quo when it comes to the areas of politics, religion, and science.[26]

THE REVEAL

The author and journalist who made these predictions was an American citizen named James Rorty.

Born in 1890, in Middleton, New York, James Rorty was educated at Tufts College in Boston. After college, he served in World War I (WWI) as an ambulance driver. When he returned to the states, he became a journalist and "ran a dry-goods business."[27] An aspiring poet, he spent his life writing newspaper articles and published a few books—two of which contained strong predictions about where the political climate of his day would lead in terms of American politics and society. James's coauthor for *McCarthy*

24. McCumber clarifies: "I am not arguing that the McCarthy era is somehow responsible for the existence of Analytic Philosophy . . . . It has a longer and honorable history, beginning well before the McCarthy era with the work of Gottlob Frege . . . and passing over to the Cambridge of Bertrand Russell at the close of the nineteenth century. But it never had the kind of dominance in its homeland—Germany—that its transplanted varieties enjoyed elsewhere" (McCumber, *TD*, 53).

25. See Plato's *Apology*.

26. See McCumber, *TD*, 59–90.

27. Gross, *RR*, 36.

and the Communists was the journalist Moshe Decter, who worried about the similarities between the American Midwest and Germany under Hitler.[28] Moshe Decter was Jewish, but Rorty had no religious affiliation.

James Rorty married Winifred Rauschenbusch, the daughter of the Baptist theologian Walter Rauschenbusch. While it seems that James Rorty never had a religious affiliation, Winifred left her Christian faith because of the neglect she felt from her overly busy father. They both identified as communists early in their marriage but changed their mind about communism because of the treatment of Trotsky by the communists in Russia.[29] They were part of an intellectual elite within New York and considered themselves "political radicals" throughout their life together.[30]

The five-year-old son, who scribbled "New York: Where Life Is Better" in a letter to his father, was their only child, Richard Rorty. Winifred birthed Richard on October 4, 1931, in New York City. They remained in New York throughout most of Richard's childhood. At the age of fourteen, Richard entered the University of Chicago as an undergraduate student. He received two degrees from the University of Chicago: a BA and an MA, both in philosophy. After Chicago, he went to Yale and earned his PhD in philosophy. He taught at Princeton University, the University of Virginia, and Stanford University. Richard died on June 8, 2007, in Palo Alto, California.

Defending both popular and unpopular positions—such as Leftism, liberalism, patriotism, postmodernism, and pragmatism—Richard Rorty is now known as one of the most important philosophers in American history.[31] Part of what turned him into one of the most important philosophers in American history is that he diagnosed and dismissed the school of thought known as "Analytic Philosophy"—not on the grounds that it resulted from McCarthyism but, rather, by using its own methods of analysis and apolitical argumentation against itself.[32] However, the connection between his father's prediction of McCarthyism leading to anti-intellectualism and Rorty's critiques of "Analytic Philosophy" should not be lost on

28. See Gross, *RR*, 58.

29. For details pertaining to the Rortys' relationship with Trotsky, see Rorty's TWO.

30. For more details, see Gross, *RR*, 29–83.

31. For one judgment among many that attempt to capture Rorty's importance, Mark Edmundson introduces Rorty on these terms: "Richard Rorty is America's most controversial philosopher. His books . . . defend the possibility of durable ethical and political allegiances that do not ground themselves in transcendental truths" (Edmundson, "Richard Rorty," 30).

32. See Rorty's *Philosophy and the Mirror of Nature*.

us; in chapter 1, therefore, I connect Richard Rorty's philosophical thinking back to his father's book on McCarthyism.

WHY THE DARK YEARS?

Like his father, Richard Rorty made predictions about American politics and society. In relation to his father's work, however, Richard Rorty articulates *when* life is better—not *where* life is better. If Rorty articulates when life is better, then why the title of *The Dark Years?*

The Dark Years? is about Richard Rorty's predictions. I am interested also in the nature of predicting the future. Usually, we think of predictions through the lenses of either religion or science. Prophecy is the religious category for the nature of predictions. Within the natural sciences, scientists use current evidence to forecast what might happen in the future if we continue down a similar path that we have been traveling. Part of Richard Rorty's work involves divorcing philosophy from both religion and science. There might be a tradition within journalism concerning making predictions about politics and society (as James Rorty does), but philosophers tend to be skeptical about making predictions.[33]

Richard Rorty, himself, illustrates the overall skepticism within philosophy about making predictions. In "Failed Prophecies, Glorious Hopes," Rorty finds it reasonable to dismiss *all* of the arguments found in both the New Testament and *The Communist Manifesto* simply because the predictions that both texts make about the future—God's return to earth in the New Testament and a classless, egalitarian society in the case of *The Communist Manifesto*—have yet to come true.[34] On Rorty's reasoning, in that particular essay, the failure of one prediction renders the whole system of thought faulty.[35]

Despite his skepticism about making predictions, Richard Rorty follows in his father's footsteps and offers predictions about America's political and social future. Richard Rorty's predictions concern the period in which we are now in as I write this book (2014–2020). However, he does not stop there: he also predicts what life in America will look like from 2020 to 2044 and from 2045 through 2095. In the year 1997, Rorty predicted the election

33. From here forward, the last name "Rorty"—when used by itself—refers to Richard Rorty and not his father James Rorty.

34. This essay can be found in Rorty, *PSH*, ch. 14.

35. For my full analysis of this essay, see Goodson, *SM*, ch. 10.

of a "strongman" in the 2016 US presidential race. Instead of waiting over twenty years to make another prediction, like his father did, Rorty's next set of predictions came a year later. In 1998, he predicted the proliferation of gun violence and an increase in mass shootings from 2014 to 2044. In both 1997 and 1998, Rorty reflects upon how homophobia, racism, and sexism will come to define American politics and society in the middle part of the twenty-first century. He labels the years from 2014 to 2044 as the "dark years" of American society. Also in 1998, however, he predicts that American politics and society will be defined eventually by (Pauline) love and (Millian) sympathy from the years 2045 to 2095.[36]

In this book, I explain and evaluate Rorty's predictions concerning the years 2014–2095. I find this exploration worthy because Rorty's predictions lead us back, conceptually, to thinking through the significance of hope.[37] While I explain and evaluate Rorty's predictions concerning the years 2014–2095 in the first part of this book, in parts two and three I think through the significance of hope—both agreeing and disagreeing with Rorty's writings on hope and how hope relates to social life.

Three important points need to be made up front about Rorty's predictions. First, his timeline is not always clear.[38] Clarity comes only through the rational reconstruction of a variety of arguments found in three different texts: *Achieving Our Country: Leftist Thought in Twentieth-Century America* (1997), *Philosophy and Social Hope* (1998), and *The Future of Religion* (2005). In this book, through the rational reconstruction of a variety of Rorty's arguments, I do my best to clarify Rorty's predictions and his timeline concerning the twenty-first century.

While many of Rorty's predictions have come true (shockingly), the second important point is that he has already missed the mark with other predictions. I present both what he gets right and what he gets wrong. In other words, I avoid the fallacy of cherry-picking in my presentation of Rorty's set of predictions. Does the failure of some of his predictions render

---

36. As in Paul of Tarsus (St. Paul or the apostle Paul) and John Stuart Mill.

37. In this way, *The Dark Years?* serves as a needed sequel—at the political and social levels—to *Strength of Mind: Courage, Hope, Freedom, Knowledge.*

38. In some lectures and previous publications, I have claimed that Rorty predicts forty years of darkness—Rorty also says forty years in at least one publication. However, the math does not work for this because he is rather clear that 2045 will be the year that marks the absolute end of the "dark years." My hunch is that Rorty used forty years for rhetorical purposes because it sounds so biblical.

the whole system of Rorty's predictions faulty? I remain interested in the nature of predictions because of questions like this one.

Third, scholars of Rorty's philosophy tend to discuss his *hopes* for American society as if he thought we (Americans) could live into them during the period of Rorty's own lifetime.[39] In what will be taken as a controversial move within scholarship on Rorty's philosophy, I treat Rorty's philosophy of religion and political philosophy—both his writings *prior to* his predictions and *after* the predictions—not as a vision of hope that Rorty developed for his own time but, rather, as pieces of a greater vision for American life after the "dark years."[40] In other words: I read Rorty's defenses of Leftism, liberalism, and patriotism as what he thinks will be the case from the years 2045 to 2095.[41]

I put the word "hopes" in italics in the previous paragraph because this third point, and the emphasis on hope, provides an opportunity to state the thesis for this book. Rorty's philosophy of religion and political philosophy provide us with a type of "social hope" about what the US can and will look like—*the country we can achieve*. According to my interpretation of his work, for Rorty this "social hope" will come about only after we survive the "dark years." My claim, against Rorty, is that we can *hope* to "achieve our country" sooner—not after going through the "dark years"—but in the near future . . . as early as the 2020s. I argue that the responsibility of intellectuals and scholars, in our present moment, involves the cultivation and promotion of "social hope"—sometimes on Rorty's terms, other times against them—and this responsibility stays with us whether we avoid or continue the "dark years." Instead of using Rorty's phrase "social hope," I defend three other versions of hope: melancholic hope, pedagogical hope, and redemptive hope.

39. I, too, wrote about Rorty's neo-pragmatism in this vein. Only when planning and researching the present book did I realize that his predictions might alter the timeline for his insights concerning the philosophy of religion and political philosophy.

40. This includes Rorty's reflections on "the future of religion," which he published only two years prior to his death.

41. An obvious challenge to my third point comes in the form of one of Rorty's book titles: *An Ethics for Today.* I address this in chapter 5.

PART 1

The Predictions

IN THIS FIRST PART, I present the set of predictions Richard Rorty makes about the time period from 2014 to 2095. In order to accomplish this, I begin by discussing why Rorty faults the American academic Left for the potential election of a "strongman" in the 2016 US presidential race. This means that I start, not with Rorty's predictions about 2014–2020, but with his reflections on the failures of Leftism toward the end of the twentieth century.

Also in chapter 1, John McCumber's research (mentioned in the "Introduction") on how McCarthyism impacted American philosophy departments aids me in connecting Richard Rorty's diagnosis of the American academy back to his father's predictions. The reconstruction of Rorty's predictions requires only Rorty's book *Achieving Our Country*, with some additional footnotes to essays he wrote and interviews he gave throughout his writing career.

In chapter 2, I take on the emotionally difficult task of describing the "dark years"—which Rorty thinks take place roughly from 2014 to 2044.[1] The darkness begins in 2014, but American politics and society goes into full darkness around 2020. This reconstruction of Rorty's predictions requires bringing two of his texts together: *Achieving Our Country* and "Looking Backwards from 2096" (published in *Philosophy and Social Hope*).

1. The dedication page in this book speaks to this emotional difficulty.

For chapter 3, I play with Rorty's predictions and make the argument that the US goes through a process of re-enchantment that leads us out of the "dark years" and offers a glimpse of American social life from 2045 to 2095. In chapter 3, I focus on Rorty's "Looking Backwards from 2096" where he predicts what will happen in the middle part of the twenty-first century. Based on my rational reconstruction of his argument, the process of exiting the "dark years" looks like this: (1) turning to literary narratives will reshape our imagination; (2) this produces a sense of shame; (3) this shame turns into sympathy; and (4) this sympathy impacts the attitudes and thoughts of American citizens. I call this re-enchantment because the transformation of shame into sympathy seems a magical one—especially in relation to thinking about how shame usually leads to fear, not sympathy.

Chapter 1

Predictions about the Already
Why We Elected a "Strongman" as POTUS

Richard Rorty's *Achieving Our Country: Leftist Thought in Twentieth-Century America* offers a strong indictment against the *modus operandi* of American politics. His target: the Left. More precisely, he targets the academic Left. Rorty's *Achieving Our Country*, therefore, is to Leftism what Thomas Frank's *What's the Matter with Kansas? How Conservatives Won the Heart of America* is to the Right.[1] In short, the academic Left ought to be faulted for failing to achieve the country that the Left claimed it wanted to achieve.

THE FALL OF THE ACADEMIC LEFT

Rorty makes three indictments against the academic Left. First, the academic Left allowed the so-called "culture wars" to become prioritized over politics. Rorty writes, "Leftists in the academy have permitted cultural politics to supplant real politics, and have collaborated with the Right in making cultural issues central to public debate."[2] The academic Left plays the "culture war" game as much as the Right does, and this means that the academic Left gave us no political vision outside of the agenda and rhetoric of the "culture wars."

---

1. In fact, in my course PHIL 331: Political Philosophy, I usually teach these two books together.

2. Rorty, *AOC*, 14.

Second, the academic Left failed to propose political projects that could bring people together. In Rorty's words, "The academic Left has no projects to propose to America, no vision of a country to be achieved by building a consensus on the need for specific reforms."[3] In essence, the academic Left gave up on making and thinking about policy and policy proposals. The academic Left played the role of critic toward political proposals, made by various politicians, but ceased offering directions or guidance for better policies.

Third, the development of "identity politics" by the academic Left committed major sins of omission.[4] Rorty seemingly praises "identity politics" but then brings a hammer down against it:

> [T]he academic Left believes [that] we must teach Americans to recognize otherness. To this end, leftists have helped . . . put together such academic disciplines as women's history, black history, gay studies, Hispanic-American studies, and migrant studies . . . . Whereas the top-down initiatives of the Old Left tried to help people who were humiliated by poverty and unemployment . . . , the top-down initiatives of the post-Sixties [academic] left have been directed toward people who are humiliated for reasons other than economic status. Nobody is setting up a program in unemployed studies, homeless studies, or trailer-park studies, because the unemployed, the homeless, and residents of trailer parks are not "other" in the relevant sense. To be other in this sense you must bear an ineradicable stigma, one which makes you a victim of socially accepted sadism rather than merely economic selfishness.[5]

On the one hand, in the name of *otherness*, the academic Left waged battles against homophobia, racism, sexism, and xenophobia. Yet, on the other hand, the academic Left has completely forgotten about and neglected the alienation—the *otherness*—of the unemployed and the working poor.[6]

3. Rorty, *AOC*, 15.

4. I call these sins of omission as a way to make sense of what the back of *Achieving Our Country* emphasizes: "Must the sins of America's past poison its hope for the future?"

5. Rorty, *AOC*, 80–81.

6. Culture critic Stephen Metcalfe writes: "Rorty's only issue with identity politics was that the Left, having worked so hard to transfer stigmatic cruelty away from received categories like race and gender, had done too little to prevent that stigma from landing on class—and that the white working class, finding itself abandoned by both the free-market right and the identity left, would be all too eager to transfer that stigma back to minorities, immigrants, gays, and coastal élites" (Metcalfe, "Rorty's Argument for National Pride").

Although the first two indictments are important, I wish to linger on this third point a bit longer because it turns out to be the one that matters most for Rorty's set of predictions.[7] Rorty argues that one of the causes of neglecting the poor relates to the shift from Marxism to Freudianism as the critical lens to see the world within the academy.[8] Because Marxism was the critical lens for seeing the world, "the Old Left tried to help people . . . humiliated by poverty and unemployment."[9] In *Achieving Our Country*, Rorty claims that the academic Left shifted from Marx's philosophy to Freud's psychoanalysis as the primary framework for making judgments about the world. I think Rorty is right about this overall, but interestingly it does not apply to philosophy departments in the United States.[10] More on this later.

Rorty distinguishes between the "reformist Left" and the "New Left" as a way to retrieve certain features of the former and make judgments against the latter.[11] Rorty critiques the "New Left" in terms of this shift from Marxism to Freudian psychoanalysis:

7. Rorty, too, lingers on this point in an interview he gives after the publication of *Achieving Our Country*: "The dream of the [academic] Left, particularly after [it gave up on] Marxism . . . , is that we can integrate all of our concerns into a single consolidated vision. But . . . we can't. We have to say one thing to one audience at one time and other things to other audiences at other times" (Rorty, *Against Bosses, Against Oligarchies*, 43). After the next question, Rorty clarifies his point about identity politics and the working poor: "And the danger of the academy's concentration on race and gender is that white workers think they are being neglected by the academy . . . , [and they are right]. The white workers *are* being neglected" (Rorty, *Against Bosses, Against Oligarchies*, 44).

8. Ellen Shrecker backs up Rorty's claim in her book *Many Are the Crimes: McCarthyism in America*, which was published around the same time as *Achieving Our Country*. She writes, "The academy lost its critical edge. College teachers embraced a cautious impartiality that in reality supported the status quo"; the critical lens used that continued the American status quo through teaching and thinking was "psychoanalysis" (Shrecker, *Many Are the Crimes*, 404–5).

9. Rorty, *AOC*, 80.

10. Philosophy departments kicked Marx out of the Western canon and never adopted Freud into its canon. Unfortunately, philosophy departments went the route of the safest possible option: Analytic Philosophy. Analytic Philosophy not only shies away from taking poverty or sexuality seriously, but it also seeks to de-legitimize philosophers who teach and write in ways that engage culture, politics, and society. In some ways, I see my own writing career as thinking through and utilizing the work of those philosophers excluded from the philosophical canon according to Analytic Philosophy.

11. Steven A. Miller emphasizes how Rorty's critique of the "New Left" includes a critique of himself as well: "In *Achieving Our Country*, he [Rorty] gives a history of American leftism and then struggles to understand why the contemporary left seems so vacuous and inefficacious compared to similar movements of yesteryear. The central difficulty he identifies is that whereas the earlier left was interested in boots-on-the-ground

> With this . . . substitution of Freud for Marx as a source of social theory, sadism rather than selfishness has become the principal target of the Left. The heirs of the New Left . . . have created, within the academy, a cultural Left. Many members of this Left specialize in what they call the "politics of difference" or "[politics] of identity" or "[politics] of recognition." This cultural Left thinks more about stigma than about money, more about deep and hidden psychosexual motivations than about shallow and evident greed.[12]

The "New Left," within the academy, chose to go the route of defending the sexuality and sexual practices of all citizens instead of using academic journals and the college classroom to raise questions about the plight of the poor in the US. What Rorty refers to as "sadism" in this passage relates to the way in which the academic Left made it their primary task to critique those who are critical of the personal sexual preferences of American citizens. In other words, the academic Left sought to out-shame those who shame citizens who identify as LGBTQ+—of course, this acronym was not yet in play in the 1970s. The academic Left went this particular route at the expense of allowing greed and selfishness to go unchecked by the American academy.[13] Why did the American Left take this route? Rorty actually does not give an answer to this question, but the answer can be captured in the phrase "academic McCarthyism."[14]

Marxism and McCarthyism

The shift away from Marxism in the academic Left is the result of McCarthyism. So argues John McCumber in two illuminating books: *The*

---

political action, more recent movements have instead limited themselves to narrow cultural battles, including about *how we talk*. His central worry is that contemporary leftists, on the whole, 'do not want to take charge of the government, only of the English department' . . . . Rorty himself was part of this problem, but he had the advantage of *realizing* it was a problem" (Miller, *Community and Loyalty*, 107).

12. Rorty, *AOC*, 76–77.

13. Rorty puts it this way: "It is as if the American Left could not handle more than one initiative at a time—as if it either had to ignore stigma in order to concentrate on money, or vice versa" (Rorty, *AOC*, 83).

14. Presidential historian David Nichols thinks this phrase is misleading because it suggests that Joseph McCarthy himself cared about and policed academic professionals. Nichols is right, of course, that McCarthy neither cared about nor policed academic professionals. However, I find the phrase accurate and powerful—which I explain and defend in what follows.

Philosophy Scare: The Politics of Reason in the Early Cold War and *Time in a Ditch: American Philosophy and the McCarthy Era*. I supplement his narrative with other research sprinkled throughout this disheartening but fascinating story.

According to McCumber, the 1950s turned out to be the decade that determined scholarship and teaching for some time in the American academy. McCumber argues, "[T]he United States had undertaken . . . the greatest intellectual purge in the history of Western democracy. This purge—carried out [in] the McCarthy era—hit academia around 1949 and did not fully subside until about 1960."[15] This judgment seems extreme.[16] A greater intellectual purge than what occurred in Nazi Germany twenty years earlier? A greater intellectual purge than the Roman Catholic Church's response to the rise of Lutheranism and Protestantism? McCumber constructs a well-researched narrative that affirms this question: yes, for over ten years, colleges and universities made decisions concerning employment and tenure on the terms of a senator from Wisconsin named Joseph McCarthy.[17]

McCumber's narrative becomes significant for understanding the 2016 presidential election because it demonstrates why professors and scholars quit caring and talking about the plight of the poor in the US. According to Richard Rorty, this lack of care and concern from academics led the working poor, uneducated, and unemployed to look for a "strongman" to vote for in the 2016 presidential election. The academy gave up on thinking about poverty, so the working poor and unemployed looked to an anti-elitist, anti-intellectual, wealthy "strongman."

15. McCumber, *TD*, 17–18.

16. Susan Jacoby concludes that this judgment is extreme because of the use of the word, "purge": "On the left, some journalists and historians use loaded words like 'purges' to describe the firings of college teachers . . . during the late forties and fifties. I find this metaphor . . . offensive and inaccurate [because a] purge is, by definition, something permanent: the Stalinist purges of 1937–38 condemned millions to death, either by immediate execution or starvation and hard labor in the Gulag" (Jacoby, *Age of American Unreason*, 96). In this chapter, I will not use the verb "purge" to describe how colleges and universities operated during the McCarthy era; however, I allow McCumber's judgment to stand that—in terms of fearfulness and numbers of faculty fired—it ranks as one of the highest "purges" in the academic context.

17. However, McCumber warns his readers: "[F]ocusing on Senator McCarthy localizes the damage even more, to the depredations of one man and to the city in which he worked—Washington, DC, In fact, the transformations in American society triggered during the McCarthy Era went beyond the Senator, beyond Washington, and indeed beyond the federal government altogether" (McCumber, *PS*, 17).

Academic McCarthyism and American Scholarship

John McCumber's phrase "academic McCarthyism" designates the initial strategy to remove "Communists from the teaching positions."[18] This strategy, however, grew to threaten "both intellectual and personal freedom, because it elevated association into guilt."[19] Within academic life, it became unclear "whether McCarthyism is best construed as anti-Communism" or "as an exercise in semi-fascistic conformism with (like Fascism itself) a core rhetoric of anti-Communism."[20] Academic McCarthyism is not about actual communists but about enforcing "conformism" at every possible level.[21]

In this sense, academic McCarthyism bred the exact opposite conditions required for living and thinking that Ralph Waldo Emerson envisioned in his essay "Self-Reliance." Academic McCarthyism threatens and violates Emerson's standards for American scholarship. On the basis of this conceptual connection, the thesis that emerges in this section is: academic McCarthyism makes it impossible to do American scholarship on the terms envisioned by Emerson. Emerson's essay "The American Scholar" represents what Supreme Court Justice Oliver Wendell Holmes Jr. calls the American "Intellectual Declaration of Independence,"[22] and his essay "Self-Reliance" presents the problems of conformism developed and found within the McCarthy era.

Emerson argues that to be a thoughtful human is to be "a nonconformist."[23] Emerson continues, "He [or she] who would gather im-

18. McCumber, *TD*, 19.

19. McCumber, *TD*, 19.

20. McCumber, *TD*, 20.

21. Through correspondence, presidential historian David Nichols offers the following clarification: "The 1950s (1950–1954) were clearly the time of McCarthy's personal influences, but the anti-intellectual mindset preceded and continued many years after his death. McCarthy died in 1957 but anti-communism, including pressures on academic life, continued for decades and afflicted academia with the House of UnAmerican Activities Committee. The issues of freedom of speech and academic inquiry are real ones, but they take different forms in different times. The results of the situation cannot be ignored in post-Joe McCarthy contexts" (Nichols, correspondence with the author, March 27, 2019). It seems that Nichols's preference involves calling it academic anti-communism instead of academic McCarthyism, but in my mind "McCarthyism" suggests more than anti-communism: it claims anti-communism as its motivation but does not limit its targets to communists.

22. See Cheever, *American Bloomsbury*, 80.

23. I am grateful for Jonathan Malesic helping me better word this sentence through a Twitter interaction on March 10, 2019.

mortal palms must not be hindered by the name of goodness, but must explore if it be goodness. Nothing is at last sacred but the integrity of your own mind."[24] Because it became an "exercise in semi-fascistic conformism," academic McCarthyism forces conditions where professors and scholars lose the integrity of their "own mind." If we apply Emerson's argument in "Self-Reliance" to the vision he articulates for American scholarship, then we might make the following inference: part of balancing knowledge—in the trivium of Nature, Tradition, Human Activity—concerns having plenty of sources to draw from in order to avoid intellectual conformity.[25] Academic McCarthyism shuts down this possibility because it limits both the sources and the use of those sources in relation to one's own scholarly integrity. Playing off Hilary Putnam's claim, "illogical thought is not . . . thought at all"[26]: conformist thinking is not thinking at all.

Some American citizens, who were intellectuals but not part of academic life, saw academic McCarthyism differently than my own connection to Emersonianism. One argument, offered during the 1950s, claimed that the problem concerns how much secrecy—not conformism—it required among academics.

This is where James Rorty makes his return into my story. McCumber writes, "James Rorty (father of Richard) argued [that] those who seek to impose their ideas in secrecy, by force rather than open argument, cannot consistently give allegiance to the community of scholars and have no place in it."[27] With this argument, James Rorty seems to be critiquing both sides: the conditions brought about by McCarthyism *and* the Left-leaning professors who succumbed to those conditions by working in secret. Mc-Cumber continues, "According to [James Rorty's] view, no ideas should be forbidden, and advocacy of even the most unpopular of them should be protected."[28] The problem with the type of secrecy that McCarthyism bred and mandated was due not only to the "witch hunt" it instigated;[29] it also

---

24. Emerson, "Self-Reliance," 132–52.

25. For my explanation of this trivium, see Goodson, *SM*, ch. 2.

26. Putnam, *Words and Life*, 247.

27. McCumber, *TD*, 19.

28. McCumber, *TD*, 19.

29. I use the phrase "witch hunt" in relation to the connection made by Charles Taylor between McCarthyism and medieval styles of policing thought: "[T]here can be a certain kind of tremendous fear when what we identify as crucial to this social order is being undermined. I mean what is crucial to achieve whatever protection we need . . . . [T]his kind of fear survives into the secular age . . . ; think of the over-reaction in the

failed to rid the academy of actual communists. It might help to remember that James Rorty had a change of heart from communism to socialism because of the Soviet treatment of Leon Trotsky. McCarthyism pushed actual American communists into further clandestine activities, which made it more difficult to eliminate the professors who needed to be removed. James Rorty thought academics should be more public about their arguments and ideas, thereby warranting their protection as academics; he also wanted to make it possible to have more certainty about who was communist and who was not.

What were the arguments and ideas—or what McCumber refers to as scholarly traits—that made McCarthyites nervous about professors and scholars? There seemed to be two traits, the elimination and suppression of which can be seen as responsible for changes within the academy that ultimately give rise to the failures of the academic Left—the same failures, it turns out, that Richard Rorty claims will lead to the results of the 2016 presidential election.

The first trait that academic McCarthyites worried about was professors and scholars who narrated the "failures during the Depression" as failures of capitalism.[30] According to academic McCarthyism, in no way should it be suggested that the American Great Depression resulted from or reveals a problem—or even a limitation—with capitalism. In this way, academic McCarthyism significantly limits professors in economics, history, law, philosophy, political science, and sociology. To ask "What can we learn from the American Great Depression?" would have been a question that must be asked by any professor or scholar with an ounce of integrity. Their answer, however, could not relate to learning about the failures of capitalism because such an answer resembles communism.

The second trait tells us why the academic Left quit talking and teaching about the plight of the unemployed and the working poor. The second trait involves showing "sympathy for the impoverished majority of human beings."[31] Academic McCarthyism targeted professors and scholars who showed "sympathy" for those who live in poverty, both in the United States and around the globe. To even talk, teach, or write about the poor

McCarthy era to the idea that some hitherto trusted milieux harboured Communists. It is perhaps for analogous reasons to these that the late Middle Ages and early modern period sees an intensification of the persecution of marginals . . . . The hunt for witches steadily escalated" (Taylor, *A Secular Age*, 88–89).

30. See McCumber, *PS*, 73.

31. McCumber, *PS*, 73.

was considered a communist activity. Within academic McCarthyism, those living in poverty either become invisible or identified as the enemy: invisible because they can be neither discussed nor mentioned; the enemy because capitalism—as I have written elsewhere—"makes poverty a problem to solve—indeed, another 'them' to eliminate through political and social policies—rather than persons [to serve]."[32] My initial intention in making that claim concerned the dichotomy between what it means to be *a problem to solve* vs. *persons to serve*.[33] When poverty becomes and remains a problem to solve, then those persons who actually live in poverty take on the status of enemy—whether consciously or subconsciously—because political and social policies aim to ease their plight or situation by eliminating *them*.[34]

Returning to the passage quoted before from Emerson's "Self-Reliance," capitalism makes it difficult to follow Emersonian wisdom about serving the poor: "[D]o not tell me, as a good man did today, of my obligation to put all poor men in good situations. Are they *my* poor?"[35] The Emersonian emphasis concerns the word "my": "There is a class of persons to whom by all spiritual affinity I am bought and sold; for them I will go to prison, if need be."[36] Oftentimes, this passage gets interpreted as Emerson refusing to help the poor because they lack "self-reliance"; this passage gets misinterpreted as a defense of the cliché that those living in poverty ought to "pull themselves up by their own bootstraps."

On the one hand, yes, Emerson thinks that the poor should have self-reliance—which should be taken neither as a negative judgment that "poor men" somehow lack self-reliance nor that poverty necessarily results from such a lack. On the other hand, and more to the point of the passage when read in the context of avoiding conformism or breaking the habit of conformity, Emerson's wisdom for readers concerns developing an awareness

---

32. Goodson, "Pedagogical Hope," para. 30.

33. Chapter 7 republishes some of the material from the previously cited essay, which means that I circle back around to the argument mentioned here.

34. In response to this paragraph, Morgan Elbot astutely points out: "[A] commitment to preserving capitalism sets up the situation where those who are evidence of its failures threaten it by undermining the beneficent image of capitalism. This threat to the professed status quo underlines the need to malign and denigrate those who live in poverty—holding them, and not capitalism, as responsible for their poverty" (Elbot, correspondence with the author, March 17, 2019).

35. Emerson, "Self-Reliance," 35.

36. Emerson, "Self-Reliance," 35–36.

for those *whom* you serve and *why* you serve them: do you serve *them* out of mere external obligation, or do you serve *them* because you have taken them on as *yours*?[37]

The most basic distinction that over-simplifies Emersonian Transcendentalism involves external obligation vs. internal conviction.[38] Professors and scholars ought to teach and write about societal obligations toward the working poor and the unemployed. They must, in other words, play the role of "the good man"—found in Emerson's paragraph—toward their readers and students. The "poor" will be cared for and considered in the most helpful and prudential ways only when the "they" become a "*my*." Under capitalism, this shift in pronouns becomes difficult because policies aimed at helping the working poor and the unemployed in actuality seek to eliminate *them* ("they").[39]

Academic McCarthyism magnifies this aspect of capitalism. As a form of insecure yet politically potent capitalism—which, paradoxically, makes it both cowardly and reckless—academic McCarthyism renders it impossible to serve the working poor and the unemployed because any hint at the shift from *them/they* to *my/ours* turns one into a suspected communist. To suggest that any of the poor are "*my* poor" is to draw the attention of McCarthyites and to risk dismissal from one's post. For all of these reasons, academic McCarthyism annihilates the conditions necessary for professors and scholars to avoid conformity and to teach and write properly about the working poor and the unemployed. Academic McCarthyism violates the (Emersonian) standards required for American scholarship.

---

37. My interpretation follows, relies on, yet tweaks Peter Dula's interpretation of the same passage when he writes: "Emerson knows that the reason it is a wicked dollar which should be withheld is because he gives that dollar for the same reason that I do. To get out from under the gaze. And so sometimes, too, I hear Emerson as a voice of bitter anger, and want to say that only someone who has felt the gaze of the poor, understood their demand, could react with such flippancy or vehemence. And those happy liberals who despise that line are the ones who can either ignore the beggars with aplomb or think a dime is supererogatory (or both). I am haunted by his [Emerson's] question 'Are they *my* poor?' Every time I give beggars money, not to be nice, not to help out, but simply to get out from under their gaze, I think with Emerson: 'Are they *my* poor?' Well, are they? Are they yours? I mean, how would I know that they are yours? How have I seen you make them yours? Or, how have we let them make us theirs?" (Dula, *Cavell, Companionship*, 29).

38. Peter Dula seems to add *guilt* to these options as well.

39. I defend this claim more fully in chapter 7.

Professors and scholars have not been serving the right people since the 1950s—not that they were serving the right people before the 1950s, but the deliberate moves against talking and teaching about the poor became ridiculous and unacademic.[40] Shame on us, and shame on colleges and universities giving in to the power and rhetoric of an insecure and manipulative senator from Wisconsin named Joseph McCarthy.

The Methods and Targets of Academic McCarthyism

While the previous section established the *that* of academic McCarthyism, the *how* and *who* of academic McCarthyism require further examination. In this section, I give a more historical account of academic McCarthyism: who did it target, and how did it conspire against these targets? This particular section ends with a lengthy discussion about one particular target of academic McCarthyism: Dr. Stanley Moore. Dr. Moore receives so much attention because his scholarly interests and projects actually provide aid and direction for the types of problems and questions that Richard Rorty thinks the academic Left dropped the ball on—so much so that, according to Rorty, it led to the working poor and unemployed looking for a "strongman" to elect in the 2016 presidential election.

In terms of the targets of academic McCarthyism, there seem to be three groups—with a fourth group seemingly suspect and simply disliked by the wrong people.[41] The three groups consisted of (1) actual communists in the American academy, (2) those who were not actual communists but given the label of a communist-sympathizer by either academic administrators, faculty colleagues, or government officials, and (3) those who were neither actual communists nor labeled as communists but made remarks in their classroom or publications that sounded communist.[42] This third group includes "people who were very far removed, both intellectually and

---

40. In his autobiographical reflections, Rorty declares that—in 1943—he became fully aware of the need to serve the poor: "I knew that poor people would always be oppressed until capitalism was overcome . . . . So at twelve I knew that the point of being human was to spend one's life fighting social injustice" (Rorty, TWO, 34–35).

41. "Targets of the McCarthyites . . . can be divided into three groups," writes McCumber (*TD*, 20).

42. In Rorty's words: "McCarthy and his people . . . said that any suggestion that capitalism needed any improvement or correction was lending aid and sympathy to the evil empire [the Soviet Union]. But, of course, that was not so" (Rorty, *Against Bosses, Against Oligarchies*, 4).

socially, from the Communist Party USA [but] had good reason to feel themselves in danger."[43] Even giving voice to certain arguments or viewpoints within the classroom made a professor susceptible to being removed from the university. One university president describes it on these terms: "[T]alking like a Communist could include saying almost anything 'provocative, unorthodox, or interesting' [in the classroom]."[44] Because of the second and third groups, but especially the third one, McCumber makes the judgment on academic McCarthyism that even assuming "a core of legitimacy to the McCarthyite movement," what cannot be denied "is that the movement quickly fell victim to excesses, both in the targets it chose and in the methods it used to pursue them."[45]

Speaking of excesses, what do I mean by a fourth group who were seemingly suspect and simply disliked by the wrong people? Depicting the pettiness and vengefulness of academic life, McCumber describes the fourth group in the following way: "[A] professor or administrator [could] use . . . charges of Communism . . . to make trouble for an unloved colleague."[46] My use of the word *seemingly* emphasizes no connection to communism but only required certain appearances, and my use of *simply* means that being disliked—"unloved" is McCumber's word—was enough ground for dismissal because of the amount of power that academic McCarthyism afforded academic administrators. Under academic McCarthyism, professors could be fired because they were disliked by administrators or more powerful colleagues. In short, academic McCarthyism represents an institution already full of pettiness and vengefulness—academic instiutions—on steroids.

How many professors and scholars actually lost their jobs because of academic McCarthyism? In terms of the first group—actual communists in the American academy—firings started happening as early as 1949. According to Ellen Shrecker, at the University of Washington,

> President Allen . . . recommended that the two Communists go
> . . . . Though he admitted that [Joseph] Butterworth and [Herbert]
> Phillips were competent scholars who had never abused their
> classrooms, he nonetheless explained that, by virtue of their party
> membership [in the Communist Party USA], they were, in his

43. McCumber, *TD*, 20.

44. McCumber, *TD*, 24.

45. McCumber, *TD*, 19.

46. McCumber, *TD*, 23.

words, "incompetent, intellectually dishonest, and derelict in their duty to find and teach the truth." The [Board of] Regents agreed and fired the three men in January 1949.[47]

The third man mentioned in the final sentence was Ralph Gundlach, dismissed because he refused to answer questions about his party affiliation. These professors were deemed "competent scholars," who maintained the integrity of their classrooms, but were fired because their association with the Communist Party USA turned them into "incompetent" scholars who lacked academic honesty and integrity.

According to Shrecker, who has made it the point of her writing career to explore the impact of McCarthyism on academic life and American culture, the University of Washington set a strong precedent for dismissing faculty. The risks were heightened because the first and second groups became hard to distinguish between (recall the second group are those who were not actual communists but given the label by either academic administrators or government officials). A piece missing from the University of Washington process but added during the 1950s involved a different "Washington": sending the accused—professors and scholars—to Washington DC for intense questioning. She writes that over "the next few years, dozens of college teachers were hauled before the main congressional investigating committees."[48] Usually, their "first hearing was in private"— which was intended as "a session designed to find out if they would cooperate with the committee."[49] Cooperating "witnesses were often released, but the unfriendlies were . . . grilled again"—yet "this time in public."[50] In terms of being fired or retained, Shrecker claims that their "fates varied": "few kept their jobs, most were fired."[51]

A Harvard administrator, Henry Rosovsky, read through Harvard's records from the 1950s and offered this stunning retrospective observation:

> Henry Rosovsky, dean of arts and sciences at Harvard from 1974 to 1984, summarized the McCarthy era as follows: "During the 1950s, a number of Harvard instructors and assistant professors became victims of McCarthy-style political pressures. Some term appointments were prematurely rescinded; a few left 'voluntarily'

47. Shrecker, "Political Tests for Professors," para. 24.
48. Shrecker, "Political Tests for Professors," para. 39.
49. Shrecker, "Political Tests for Professors," para. 39.
50. Shrecker, "Political Tests for Professors," para. 39.
51. Shrecker, "Political Tests for Professors," para. 40.

rather than facing investigation of their political opinions and affiliations. The same was true everywhere else, and I do not recall that their elders [administrators and full professors] organized an effective defense anywhere."[52]

McCumber comments on Rosovsky's observations: "McCarthy-era political pressures thwarted a number of careers, primarily those of junior professors."[53] Although *The Harvard Crimson* reports on those within the university pushing back against policing Harvard's academic life on the terms of McCarthyism, Harvard University eventually settled on this agreement with the McCarthyites: "[I]f a teacher was a Communist, he would be fired, whether he had tenure or not. But what if he *had been* a Communist or had taken the fifth amendment?"[54] According to *The Harvard Crimson*, that question remained open on purpose—the vagueness being used as leverage against all those "instructors and assistant professors" mentioned by Rosovsky.

Outside of Harvard, what was life like for new PhDs trying to begin their careers?[55] I answer this question by focusing on one professor, because his case exemplifies what young scholars should have been allowed to do in terms of research but were not afforded the freedom to do.

John McCumber introduces us to the resilient and remarkable Dr. Stanley Moore! In McCumber's words:

> Stanley Moore [1914–1997] ...joined the philosophy department at Reed College in Oregon after a job offer from Brooklyn College was rescinded [sometime between 1952–1953] because one of his letters of recommendation called him a "fanatical Marxist, both in theory and in practice."[56]

After he started teaching at Reed College, however, the Board of Trustees there called for his resignation. The faculty defended Moore's place at Reed

52. McCumber, *TD*, 18.

53. McCumber, *TD*, 18.

54. Heineman, "University in the McCarthy Era."

55. A caveat: we do not have definite numbers on how many people lost their jobs due to academic McCarthyism. In the words of Susan Jacoby, "For unknown college professors and teachers . . . , there was only vulnerability. It will never be possible to assess the toll that government investigations exacted from men and women of modest means and modest ambitions when they were faced with the same choice as those with considerable resources." She concludes with the observation that academic McCarthyism led to several professors losing their jobs—both "Harvard professor[s]" and "professor[s] at . . . state college[s]" (Jacoby, *Age of American Unreason*, 103).

56. McCumber, *TD*, 26.

College, but the Board of Trustees had the final say and removed him from the faculty. This occurred in 1954.

In a touching "Remembrance" of Dr. Moore, Monte Johnson further sets the scene in 1954. What did all of this mean for Moore's reputation? Johnson's answer:

> Stanley was a person of principle—fearless . . . and fair-minded. He became nationally famous in the profession because of his courageous stand against the encroachments of McCarthyism on academic freedom. In 1954 he lost his tenure position as Professor of Philosophy at Reed College when he refused to answer questions about his political affiliations before the House Un-American Activities Committee. In characteristically witty fashion Stanley remarked at the end of the hearings, "When this investigation started, I predicted that I would win the argument and lose the job. My prediction . . . has now been confirmed."[57]

McCumber reports that, eventually, Reed College's "board of trustees . . . admit[ted] that its action with respect to Moore had been wrong."[58] When did this admission take place? Not until 1978![59]

What was Moore's intellectual sin? He set out to teach and write on the question of the actual relationship between communism and Karl Marx's philosophy—for the purpose of defending neither communism nor Marx's philosophy but to better understand both. In other words, he sought to do the job of an academic philosopher: to think and write critically about claims, ideologies, and movements that declare their inspiration from a historical philosopher. I cannot imagine a better use of a philosopher's research and writing time, during the Cold War, than to make explicit the ways in which Soviet communism achieves or fails on the terms of the individual philosopher it claims as its inspiration and primary source: Karl Marx.

So what happened to Stanley Moore after his firing from Reed College? Monte Johnson narrates a beautiful answer to this question:

> Having been fired under these conditions, Stanley was unable to find a permanent teaching post for another decade, even though

57. Johnson, "Stanley W. Moore Remembrance."

58. See McCumber, *TD*, 26–27.

59. Additionally, a face-to-face apology was issued in . . . 1995, forty-one years after his firing—unbelievable! Monte Johnson narrates the 1995 apology: "In 1993, the president of Reed invited Stanley to visit the College, and in 1995 the last surviving member of the Board that fired Stanley expressed his regret and apologized to him" (Johnson, "Stanley W. Moore Remembrance").

he was widely regarded as one of the most knowledgeable philosophical historians in America. He did teach during the period of 1955–1965 on a part-time basis at Barnard College. During this hiatus most of his time was spent researching and writing. In 1964, the new UCSD [University of California San Diego] philosophy department, chaired by Richard Popkin and whose other members were Jason Saunders and Avrum Stroll, proposed a symposium on the topic "Marx Today." With financial support from Chancellor Herbert York and Dean Keith Brueckner, the department arranged for a three-day conference that was held in Sumner Auditorium. The main speakers were Stanley Moore, Herbert Marcuse, Lewis Feuer, and the moderator was Joseph Tussman of UC Berkeley. This conference caused a sensation on campus. It had virtually one hundred percent attendance from the scientific community. Its stars were Moore and Marcuse, and with the enthusiastic support of York and Brueckner, and such faculty members as S. J. Singer and James Arnold, we managed to hire both of them. It began an auspicious period that gave international visibility to the department.[60]

Stanley Moore authored four books (and coedited at least one book). All four books attempt to better understand capitalism, communism, and Karl Marx's relationship to both of these isms. Again, from Monte Johnson's "Remembrance":

> The first of [Stanley Moore's] works [*The Critique of Capitalist Democracy* (1957)] is more expository than critical. The latter three [*Three Tactics* (1963), *Marx and the Choice Between Socialism and Communism* (1980), and *Marx Versus Markets* (1993)] relentlessly explore a deceptively simple question: Why does Karl Marx call for the elimination not only of the inequalities he associated with capitalist private ownership but also the institution of market exchange? In other words, why does Marx envisage the ideal of humane and decent social order in the form of communist society? The issue goes to the core of Marx's intellectual legacy. Stanley Moore's writings analyze the issue with scrupulous scholarly care in the interpretation of Marx's texts, a generous sympathy with the values of solidarity and emancipation he discerned in these texts, and a rigorous intelligence directed to the exposure of Marx's mistakes and evasions that have a bearing on his historical prophecies and revolutionary urgings. Moore's conclusion is that Marx has no good arguments that should persuade us to follow him beyond

60. Johnson, "Stanley W. Moore Remembrance."

the condemnation of exploitation to the rejection of markets and exchange. For many years after his formal retirement, Moore continued his sensible and nuanced reflections as to how to extract the rational kernel of Marx's radicalism from the romantic and utopian shell in which it seemed to be encased. In his last writings he proposed a pairing of Rousseau's emphasis on economic transformation. All of Stanley Moore's writings felicitously combine the qualities of a rigorous scholar and staunch social critic.[61]

Three years after being dismissed from Reed College, Moore published his first book—which has a misleading title (perhaps deliberately misleading as a way to amp up his rebellion against academic McCarthyism). Moore's *Critique of Capitalist Democracy* explains and evaluates theories of the state from the writings of Karl Marx, Friedrich Engels, and Vladimir Lenin—with special emphasis on where each thinker locates the failure within the combination of capitalism and democracy.

Moore's next three books examine questions relating specifically to theoretical flaws and limitations within Marx's philosophy, and he also criticized the use of Marx's philosophy by and within Soviet communism. If academic philosophy were to achieve relevance during the Cold War, this type of research and writing represents exactly what academic philosophers should have been doing. Moore should have been released neither by Brooklyn College nor Reed College; rather, he should have been raised up as an exemplary philosophy professor during this time for the following reasons: (a) actually paying attention to the world around him and the world writ large, (b) basing his research on the political crisis of his day (rather than waiting for the Cold War to end and then starting to think about ways to critique both capitalism and communism), and (c) writing books that offer wisdom to his readers and students for thinking about the complex relationship between Marx's philosophy and Soviet communism.

In addition to professors like Stanley Moore, who persisted in their research and refused to conform to the new standards of academic McCarthyism, what the academy needed during the so-called McCarthy era was an academic equivalent of the journalist Edward R. Murrow. According to presidential historian David N. Nichols, Murrow "plumbed the depths of the paranoid psychology on which McCarthyism thrived."[62] Murrow stated with clarity:

61. Johnson, "Stanley W. Moore Remembrance."
62. Nichols, *Ike and McCarthy*, 188.

> We must not confuse dissent with disloyalty. We must remember always that accusation is not proof and that conviction depends upon evidence and due process of law. We will not walk in fear, one of another. We will not be driven by fear into an age of unreason, if we dig deep in our history and our doctrine, and remember that we are not descended from fearful men—not from men who feared to write, to speak, to associate and to defend causes that were, for the moment, unpopular. This is no time for men who oppose Senator McCarthy's methods to keep silent.[63]

Where were the Edward Murrows in academic life standing up *to* academic McCarthyism and standing up *on behalf of* the professors and scholars whose academic freedom(s) were being stripped away? Where were the Edward Murrows in academic life standing up *for* the need to talk and teach about the working poor and unemployed? Except for the teaching and writing of Dr. Stanley Moore, academic life never had its Edward Murrow.[64]

One Result of Academic McCarthyism: The Problem of Analytic Philosophy

Because of academic McCarthyism, academic life has been altered for the worse. McCumber even uses the word trauma for the impact academic McCarthyism had and continues to have on professors and scholars. In my judgment, this trauma remains one of the reasons why disciplines like philosophy lack relevance or even a voice within American public life.[65]

Academic McCarthyism, broadly speaking, negatively impacted the humanities and the social sciences in the American academy. McCumber claims, "In the humanities as in the social sciences, the dominance of politically narrowed mindsets prevented the recognition of changes on the horizon."[66] Within the humanities and the social sciences, multiple and various political perspectives have been narrowed and reduced.[67]

---

63. Quoted in Nichols, *Ike and McCarthy*, 187–88; I was unable to find the script at the location cited by Nichols (see Nichols, *Ike and McCarthy*, 347, fn 18).

64. Although total happenstance, Stanley Moore died the same year Richard Rorty published *Achieving Our Country* (1997).

65. In McCumber's words: "Its traumatic events explain why philosophers have isolated themselves within academia and why they are unwilling to reflect in public about [how philosophy helps public life]" (McCumber, *TD*, 18).

66. McCumber, *PS*, 21.

67. Ellen Shrecker connects this to how it impacts thinking about the poor: "The

More narrowly, academic McCarthyism left a deep and negative impact on the academic discipline of philosophy. McCumber focuses his research on the subject matters within philosophy that disappeared, for a time, because of academic McCarthyism and on how the received Western philosophical canon changed because of academic McCarthyism.

Some background to this. The usual offerings that academic philosophy departments at least attempt to maintain include a balance of the following subject matters: aesthetics, epistemology, ethics, logic, metaphysics, philosophy of mathematics, philosophy of science, political philosophy, and social philosophy (in various forms). Academic McCarthyism elevated subjects like the philosophy of mathematics, philosophy of science, and logic (especially symbolic logic) at the expense of courses and publications in political and social philosophy. According to McCumber, political and social philosophy disappeared—in terms of being taught and written about—"until reintroduced by John Rawls in 1971."[68]

In Michigan, for instance, legislation was introduced to reduce the philosophy courses offered by state-funded universities to only logic and symbolic logic.[69] This means that the state legislator attempted to play the role of "curriculum committee" on behalf of every state-funded university. The legislation failed, but the attempt demonstrates the anti-educational and anti-intellectual consequences of academic McCarthyism.[70]

The dominance of Analytic Philosophy in American philosophy departments, which results from academic McCarthyism, continues to make philosophy "safe" in terms of not challenging the cultural and political status quo.[71] In this way, Analytic Philosophy represents an anti-

---

social sciences faced . . . pressures [involving being] subject to . . . suspicion . . . . By the 1950s, social science had become . . . methodologically rigorous and ostensibly neutral. It embraced survey research and quantitative analysis. Controversial questions about class structure or the allocation of economic resources simply disappeared from the academic mainstream" (Shrecker, *Many Are the Crimes*, 406–7).

68. McCumber, *TD*, 38.

69. In McCumber's words: "In Michigan . . . , a state legislator demanded the abolition of all philosophy courses in the state universities except for those in symbolic logic and advanced symbolic logic" (McCumber, *TD*, 21).

70. For more information on how governmental skepticism—from both federal and state legislatures—toward colleges and universities led to anti-intellectualism in the US, see Jacoby's *Age of American Unreason*, ch. 4.

71. In the twenty-first century, by actively promoting Analytic Philosophy and labeling any philosopher who challenges Analytic Philosophy as illegitimate, Brian Leiter has given himself the role of policing philosophy departments and keeping philosophy "safe"

educational and even anti-intellectual mode of doing philosophy. I realize this sounds deeply counter-intuitive because Analytic Philosophy requires so much precision and rigor in thinking (both precision and rigor require intellectual virtues), but those American philosophy departments that only allowed Analytic Philosophy did so out of cowardice and a false sense of security (these represent intellectual vices).

Within the discipline of philosophy, academic McCarthyism policed out significant sources within the received Western canon. Because of academic McCarthyism, "virtually all the tentative, open, skeptical, discussions that, from Plato's aporetic dialogues on[ward], [which] have constituted much of the philosophical life [were prohibited]."[72] Academic McCarthyism forced exclusion of "the kind of moral betterment that Kant extracts from metaphysics . . . at the end of the *Critique of Pure Reason* . . . , Kierkegaardian and [other] existentialist perspectives . . . altogether . . . , [and all] critical reflection[s] on . . . social and institutional conditions."[73] Some of Plato's dialogues, Kant's first *Critique*, Kierkegaard, Nietzsche, and Heidegger: all removed from the canon of Western philosophy because of academic McCarthyism. I imagine Plato's *Republic*, especially, was troubling because it critiques the very politics that we see within McCarthyism: a politics lacking justice, prudence, and truth.

Of course, G. W. F. Hegel and Karl Marx were removed from the Western canon on account of academic McCarthyism. McCumber takes up the reasons for this in his *The Philosophy Scare*. From one perspective, the problem with the Soviet Union was that it took Hegel's and Marx's philosophies *too seriously*. The response to this problem involved neither countering their philosophies through argumentation nor conceiving of different interpretations of their philosophies in relation to the use of their theories by the Soviet Union. The response to this problem simply involved neither teaching nor treating them at all.[74]

---

in terms of not challenging the cultural and political status quo. Finnish philosopher and public intellectual Esa Saarinen goes as far as to say that Leiter's defense of Analytic Philosophy leads to cynicism (see Saarinen, "Kindness to Babies," 145–64). I should note a point of gratitude to my own *doktorvater*, Professor Peter Ochs, for steering me away from Analytic Philosophy; I imagine that neither one of us wish to be considered a "legitimate" philosopher on the standards of Analytic Philosophy, post-McCarthyism, and Brian Leiter—in particular.

72. McCumber, *TD*, 40.

73. McCumber, *TD*, 40–41.

74. McCumber reports on a Hegel scholar being fired from one university; as of 2014, this university has never hired a scholar in Hegel's philosophy again (see McCumber, *TD*, 35).

In sum, academic McCarthyism had and continues to have negative results for philosophy departments—as well as for the humanities and social sciences. It limits what can be argued, and it reduces potential sources of wisdom simply because of their (historical philosophers') association with Soviet communism. In this way, guilt by association not only threatened living professors and scholars; guilt by association also applied to past thinkers. Hegel and Marx, for instance, became anathema simply because they were used within Soviet communism as sources of inspiration and wisdom. Instead of allowing and encouraging alternative interpretations of Hegel's and Marx's philosophies through the exercise of argument and counter-argument, the philosophical canon simply was reduced.

PREDICTIONS LEADING UP TO 2016 PRESIDENTIAL ELECTION[75]

Between John McCumber's (and others') research on the impact of McCarthyism on the American academy and Rorty's critiques of the academic Left,[76] the reasons why American Leftism abandoned the poor have been established.[77] Rorty predicts the consequences of these Leftist failures for the twenty-first century.[78]

75. Parts of this section are republished from Goodson, SM, ch. 10.

76. In an interview given after *Achieving Our Country*, Rorty too reflects upon "academic McCarthyism"—though he calls it "McCarthyite culture." He says, "McCarthy somehow managed to get anti-communism front and center and scared the life out of everybody. He gave anti-communism a bad name" (Rorty, *Against Bosses, Against Oligarchies*, 3).

77. Ellen Shrecker perhaps says it most clearly when she writes, "If nothing else, McCarthyism destroyed the left." She continues, "As we assess the consequences of McCarthyism's assault on the left, we encounter a world of things that did not happen: reforms that were never implemented, unions that were never organized, movements that never started, books that were never published, films that were never produced. And questions that were never asked. We are, in short, looking at 'might have beens' and at a wide range of political and cultural possibilities that did not materialize. We are also looking at a lost moment of opportunity, when in the immediate aftermath of [WWII] the left-labor coalition that McCarthyism destroyed might have offered an alternative to the rigid pursuit of the Cold War and provided the basis for an expanded welfare state" (Shrecker, *Many Are the Crimes*, 369).

78. Rorty died prior to the election of Barack Obama as POTUS, but the only aspect of Obama's presidency that might have impacted Rorty's predictions is the reaction to Obama's skin color and the "birther movement." None of these factors are accounted for in Rorty's predictions.

Rorty sets up his predictions about the 2016 presidential election with two observations concerning the end of the twentieth century. First, "the choice between the two major [political] parties has come down to a choice between cynical lies and terrified silence."[79] According to Rorty, the Republican Party has made a habit of "cynical lies" whereas the Democratic Party stands in "terrified silence."[80]

Second, Rorty observes that the fact of globalization leads to two very different responses: one from college educated American citizens and another from non-college-educated American citizens. Labeling college educated American citizens as "intellectuals," Rorty comments: "[We] intellectuals . . . are ourselves quite well insulated . . . from the effects of globalization. To make things worse, we often seem more interested in the workers of the developing world than in the fate our fellow [uneducated] citizens."[81]

These two observations lead Rorty to his predictions about the conditions leading up the 2016 presidential election.[82] First, Rorty predicts "populist movements are likely to overturn constitutional governments."[83] They will make anti-globalization, anti-labor union, and anti-taxation their main political stances. Second, Rorty predicts "the members of labor unions, and unorganized unskilled workers, will sooner or later realize that their government is not even trying to prevent wages from sinking or to prevent jobs from being exported."[84] Third, Rorty predicts that white suburbanites will "pull up the drawbridge behind them" because "although social mobility had been appropriate for their parents," they decide not to allow it "to the next generation."[85] Fourth, Rorty predicts a kind of despair about the relationship between "unskilled workers" and "white-collared workers": "the members of labor unions, and unorganized unskilled workers" will come to the realization "that suburban white-collar workers . . . are

---

79. Rorty, AOC, 87.

80. Rorty spends the majority of the book critiquing the Left, not the Right.

81. Rorty, AOC, 89.

82. In SM, I articulated three of Rorty's predictions leading up to the presidential election; I now find that he makes five predictions leading up to the presidential election.

83. Rorty, AOC, 89.

84. Rorty, AOC, 89.

85. Rorty, AOC, 86.

not going to let themselves be taxed to provide social benefits for anyone else."[86]

Lastly, the lack of raises for cost of living for all citizens middle-class and lower—which goes back to the 1970s—will turn economic anxiety and insecurity into a way of life for an overwhelming majority of Americans:[87]

> The question . . . is whether the average married couple, both working full time, will ever be able to take home [enough] to permit home ownership or buy decent daycare. In a country that believes neither in public transportation nor in national health insurance, this income permits a family of four only a humiliating, hand-to-mouth existence. Such a family . . . will be constantly tormented by fears of wage rollbacks and downsizing, and of the disastrous consequences of even a brief illness.[88]

Instead of claiming that Rorty is right in some general way about this final prediction before the 2016 presidential election, I can say that—despite being off by $10,000[89]—Rorty describes my own "family of four" exactly right.[90]

86. Rorty, AOC, 89–90.

87. In an essay written in 1993, Rorty marks 1973 as the year of decline in American economic history: "At the moment [1993] there [is a] cultural war . . . being waged in the United States. The . . . war is important. It will decide whether our country continues along the trajectory defined by the Bill of Rights, the Reconstruction Amendments, the building of the land-grant colleges, female suffrage, the New Deal, *Brown vs. Board of Education*, the building of community colleges, the feminist movement, and the gay rights movement. Following this trajectory would mean that America will continue to set an example of increasing tolerance and equality. But it may be that this trajectory could be maintained only while Americans' average real income continued to rise. So 1973 may have been the beginning of the end: the end both of rising economic expectations and of the political consensus that emerged from the New Deal" (Rorty, TWO, 45–46).

88. Rorty, AOC, 83–84.

89. Rorty predicts $30,000 will be the average salary for a family of four where both parents work full-time.

90. Without help from three different sources in 2013, we could not pay the medical bills that came after I suffered a stroke. Without those sources of financial help, I am uncertain what would have happened to us in terms of dealing with collection agencies and perhaps filing for bankruptcy. Those three sources prevented such dire consequences, but not every family in our position can draw from multiple sources for financial help. Additionally, we have stated over and over within our family how much of a burden it is to require two cars—with two car payments (until my elderly grandmother gifted us her car)—in order to have a non-chaotic existence in the Midwestern part of the United States. More public transportation, especially in the Midwestern part of the United States, would help families out more than any governmental calculation can guess. We live paycheck to paycheck, which is our way to say that we have a "hand-to-mouth

With all of these conditions in place, in the 2016 presidential election . . .

"Something Will Crack"[91]

In 1997, Richard Rorty predicts the 2016 presidential election:

> At that point, something will crack. The nonsuburban electorate
> will decide that the system failed and start looking around for a
> strongman to vote for—someone willing to assure them that, once
> he is elected, the smug bureaucracy, tricky lawyers, overpaid bond
> salesmen, and postmodernist professors will no longer be calling
> the shots.[92]

This passage from *Achieving Our Country* went viral on November 9,
2016—the day after the presidential election![93]

Rorty's prediction is followed by the ironic claim, "For once such a
strongman takes office, nobody can predict what will happen."[94] Ironic, because Rorty makes several more predictions! I limit this particular chapter
to Rorty's predictions, found in *Achieving Our Country*, about what happens once this "strongman" gets elected. The next two chapters consider
Rorty's predictions found in *Philosophy and Social Hope* (published a year
after *Achieving Our Country*) concerning the long-term effects of the 2016
presidential election.

With the election of this "strongman," Rorty predicts a severe regression in the way we talk and think about African Americans and
Mexican Americans, gays and lesbians, and women. With the election of
this "strongman," Rorty says, "the gains made in the past forty years by

---

existence." Within the academy, more money is required to earn one's graduate degrees
because of increases in tuition costs since the early 2000s; however, faculty salaries have
not increased as much percentage-wise as tuition costs have. So professors-in-training
pay more for their graduate degrees, but when they finally find a faculty position they get
paid nearly the same salary as professors who got their degrees before all of the tuition
hikes (even though our students are paying much more in tuition). We require a lot
of financial help to survive—because of the amount of our salaries and because of the
enormous costs we have in relation to car payments, health insurance, mortgage for our
house, professional obligations, and student loans.

91. Parts of this section are republished from Goodson, *SM*, ch. 10.

92. Rorty, *AOC*, 90.

93. See https://twitter.com/search?q=2016%20richard%20rorty%20achieving%20
our%20country&src=typd.

94. Rorty, *AOC*, 90.

black and brown Americans, and by homosexuals, will be wiped out," and "[j]ocular contempt for women will come back into fashion."[95] This means that the work of the Academic Left from the past forty years will seem null and void: "All the sadism which the Academic Left has tried to make unacceptable to its students will come flooding back," and "all the resentment which badly educated Americans feel about having their manners dictated to them by college graduates will find an outlet."[96] This part of Rorty's predictions ought to be judged as accurate and right.

Oligarchy or Tyranny?

In his *Republic*, Plato famously defends a cyclical pattern concerning five forms of government. We can define them roughly in the following ways:

> Aristocracy: justice belongs to the educated, political elite.
>
> Timocracy: politics involves the pursuit of honor, neither justice nor wisdom.
>
> Oligarchy: politics involves the pursuit of wealth and allowing/encouraging the wealthy to increase their wealth.
>
> Democracy: politics involves equality for all citizens, no matter the levels of education or wealth with citizens in the city.
>
> Tyranny: taking away the equality and freedom earned within democracy; tyranny occurs when one person (usually not a politician) rises to power by championing the uneducated against the political elite.

Aristocracy tends to turn into a timocracy because glory and honor become more exciting than what aristocracy has to offer. Timocracy tends to turn into an oligarchy because the timocrat(s) decide to exchange their glory and honor for property and wealth, and being wealthy eventually equates to political power. An oligarchy tends to turn into a democracy because the lower classes rise up against the wealthy elite and use their numbers to take power. A democracy tends to turn into tyranny because democracy breeds chaos and disorder, which allows for a singular individual to centralize power through rhetoric that speaks to the desires of democrats but ends with a tyrant. After a while, society returns to aristocracy because the well-educated are able to outmaneuver and outsmart the tyrant; they return to power, and the pattern starts over.

95. Rorty, *AOC*, 90.
96. Rorty, *AOC*, 90.

Assuming that—prior to 2016—the US was a functional democracy, the question becomes whether the 2016 presidential election proves Plato's cyclical pattern correct. If we were a democracy, are we now under tyranny?[97]

Rorty's predictions seem to undermine the cyclical pattern Plato lays out.[98] On Plato's terms, Rorty predicts an oligarchy instead of a tyranny: "For after my imagined strongman takes charge, he will quickly make his peace with the international superrich."[99] This will make him "a disaster for the country and the world" to the point that people all over the world "will wonder why there was so little resistance to his evitable rise."[100] Rorty does not predict tyranny and, therefore, would not think that our current POTUS is a tyrant.[101] Rather, according to Rorty's predictions, we now live in an oligarchy.[102]

Notice further that, although anti-globalization was one of the conditions for electing such a "strongman," this "strongman" is not anti-globalization. Globalization becomes defined through a powerful network of the "international superrich." The wool has been pulled over the eyes of the sheep: the sheep being those who voted for Donald J. Trump under the guise that he is anti-globalization. Trump favors globalization when it

---

97. While writing this book, I heard Jeffrey Stout give a lecture affirming this question. Stout argued that the ancient understanding of tyranny provides the best lens for understanding Donald J. Trump's presidency. See Stout, "Religion within the Bounds."

98. For some reason (he does not give one), Steven A. Miller thinks that Rorty predicts fascism in the twenty-first century: Rorty "presciently diagnosed that the twenty-first century's prime troubles would be economic, and . . . he identified an economic path by which fascism could come to America" (Miller, *Community and Loyalty*, 107).

99. Rorty, *AOC*, 91.

100. Rorty, *AOC*, 91.

101. However, in an interview, he does equate his predicted "strongman" with demagoguery: "Every once in a while fundamentalists and unscrupulous demagogues manage to break out of their cages and to whip the masses into a frenzy" (Rorty, *Against Bosses, Against Oligarchies*, 4). In the case of 2015–2016, the cage serves as a metaphor for Trump Tower; the "break out" was represented by riding down an escalator on June 16, 2015 (see Falcone's "Trump Rode an Escalator to 2016 Presidential Announcement").

102. Apparently, Rorty's friend and famous judge Richard Posner thinks Rorty worries too much about "oligarchies." At the end of an interview, Rorty reveals this: "Richard Posner has always said that philosophically I'm on the right track, it's just that I had no sense of concrete economics or socioeconomic policy: 'Rorty is still talking about "oligarchy" and "the bosses"'" (Rorty, *Against Bosses, Against Oligarchies*, 65). Perhaps the question concerning Rorty's predictions is, why is Rorty "still talking about 'oligarchy'" into the mid-twenty-first century?

comes to constructing and defending a powerful network of the "international superrich."

THE RECEPTION OF RORTY'S PREDICTIONS
FOUND IN *ACHIEVING OUR COUNTRY*

In addition to the "something will crack" passage going viral the day after the results of the 2016 presidential election, several journalists also commented on Rorty's predictions about the 2016 presidential election. I conclude this chapter by highlighting the more interesting engagements with Rorty's predictions.

First, writing for *The New York Times* a few weeks after the 2016 election results, Jennifer Senior states: "Donald J. Trump enthusiasts might dispute the word strongman, but the essence of . . . Rorty's argument holds up surprisingly well."[103] His voters might dispute the label of a "strongman," but his campaign promises are classically "strongman": as Trump claimed at the Republican National Convention in the summer of 2016, "Nobody knows the system better than me, which is why I alone can fix it."

Perhaps, in the case of Trump, "strongman" simply means having the Nietzschean ability to stir up emotions of hatred and vengefulness for the sake of then taking advantage of those who enslave themselves to you because of the hatred and vengefulness you sold to them. For instance, Trump fits R. R. Reno's description of the Nietzschean strongman:[104] "the noble strongmen of Nietzsche's imagination were indifferent to their weak slaves, indulging them now and again in *gestures of magnanimity* but *never counting them or their needs as relevant* to the ideal life."[105] I italicize parts of Reno's quotation because, on the one hand, his phrasing captures Trump's presidency as much as any two phrases can: Trump's rallies, speeches, and tweets are "gestures of magnanimity"; yet, his policies on health care, tariffs, and "the wall" make life harder for a majority of his supporters and voters—hence "never counting them or their needs as relevant."[106]

On the other hand, when it comes to Trump's relationship to his followers ("weak slaves"), I disagree with the language of "indifference"

103. Senior, "Richard Rorty's 1998 Book."
104. Ironically, Reno was also one of the most vocal Christian theologians who supported Trump's candidacy in 2016.
105. Reno, "Nietzsche's Deeper Truth."
106. Reno, "Nietzsche's Deeper Truth."

because the whole of the Trump presidency has been one of constant indulgence with his supporters. Trump cares less about policy and more about the admiration and adoration of his supporters. Attention, celebrity, and turning politics into reality television seems to be what drives and motivates Trump the most.[107] This means that all of the characteristics of the "strongman" given by Reno fit Trump, except for the characteristic of "indifference." Lacking one of the characteristics, however, does not change the fact that overall Trump fits this version of a "strongman." In this sense, we can still judge Rorty's prediction concerning the 2016 presidential election as accurate, right, and shockingly so!

The use of the phrase "shockingly so" leads to the second interesting engagement with Rorty's prediction after the 2016 presidential election. Writing for *Cosmopolitan*, Megan Friedman begins her column with this attention grabber: "Were you shocked when Donald Trump won the presidential election? If you had read this book, you wouldn't have been."[108] She concludes her brief column with anecdotal evidence about why Rorty is right, not only about the election of Trump, but Trump making "peace with the international superrich":

> Another line in the book? "After my imagined strongman takes charge, he will quickly make his peace with the international superrich." Recently, Trump met with Indian real estate developers who built the first Trump-branded buildings in the country. Did Rorty have a time machine or what?[109]

As a fan of the *Back to the Future* franchise and a scholar of Rorty's philosophy, I must admit that it gives me a lot of mental satisfaction to think of Rorty traveling with Doc Brown and Marty McFly to October 21, 2015, and then returning with them to 1985—to which 1985 I do not know!—and taking over ten years to write his predictions about the twenty-first century based on his experiences of a few days in October 2015.

Third, and challenging both Friedman's and Senior's news stories, blogger Andy Seal presents two arguments for why Rorty's predictions about the 2016 presidential election should not be taken seriously. Seal claims,

---

107. The insights in this paragraph originally came from Nicholas Detter while studying Rorty's *Achieving Our Country* in PHIL 331: Political Philosophy in Fall 2019.

108. Friedman, "Book Written in 1998 Predicted Trump's Election."

109. Friedman, "Book Written in 1998 Predicted Trump's Election."

First, Rorty's story only makes sense by leaving out materially important developments that took place between 1998 and 2016, and the omission of these events from Rorty's "prediction" fundamentally mars not only its accuracy but its explanatory power. Second—and somewhat less straightforwardly—Rorty's particular hobby-horses and distinctive temperament . . . are almost uniquely antipathetic to the role of [a] prophet [making predictions]: Rorty's peculiar understanding of history and society, his models of cultural change and human character, are not only ill-suited to prophecy [and prediction-making], but actively negate any kind of thinking which we might regard as prophetic.[110]

Seal raises two good questions, both of which I raised in the "Introduction" to this book. My argument, against Seal, is that precisely because Rorty eschews making predictions—and dismisses two whole traditions (Christianity and Marxism) for making faulty predictions—his own predictions must be taken quite seriously. Which is not to say that his predictions must be taken as absolutely right, but it requires inferences that really push against the rhetoric found in *Achieving Our Country* and *Philosophy and Social Hope* to conclude that Rorty's words "actively negate" prediction-making.

Although I will not leave *Achieving Our Country* behind in my analysis, it now seems appropriate to move on to Rorty's predictions in *Philosophy and Social Hope*.

110. Seal, "Why Richard Rorty Was Not a Prophet."

Chapter 2

Predictions about the Meantime
Thirty Years of Darkness (circa 2014–2044)

RICHARD RORTY'S ESSAY "LOOKING Backwards from the Year 2096" is nothing if not strange. It begins with fictional publication information where even the most careful reader might miss Rorty's first prediction about the twenty-first century—which is asserted but neither defended nor explained. The fictional publication information offered by Rorty states: "[the following is] in the form of an excerpt from the article on 'Fraternity' in the seventh edition of *A Companion to American Thought*, published in 2095 and edited by Cynthia Rodriguez, SJ, and Youzheng Patel."[1]

Rorty's first controversial prediction concerns the ordination of a female priest, who carries her ordination with the Society of Jesus—the Jesuits. This might be controversial but perhaps not strange. One strange aspect of this fictional bibliographical information is that the volume is published in 2095, but the title of Rorty's essay is "Looking Backward from *2096.*" Another strange aspect: when he calls this an "excerpt," he means that it comes from a *New York Times* article called "Fraternity Reigns"—which Rorty actually published in the *New York Times* on September 26, 1996![2] So when he republishes this "excerpt" in *Philosophy and Social Hope*, he envisions it in a fictional "companion" published in 2095 but merely and mistakenly adds one hundred years to the actual publication—making it

1. Rorty, *PSH*, 243.
2. Rorty, "Fraternity Reigns."

2096. This also means that when I say he made sets of predictions in 1997 and 1998, some of the predictions from 1998 were first published in the *New York Times* in 1996.

Reconstructing Rorty's predictions concerning the thirty years of darkness is my only concern within this chapter.

THE DARK YEARS

The first sentence of "Looking Backwards from the Year 2096" is sobering and somber: "Our long, hesitant, painful recovery, over the last five decades, from the breakdown of democratic institutions during the Dark Years (2014–2044) has changed our political vocabulary, as well as our sense of the relation between the moral order and the economic order."[3] The five decades refer to 2045–2095, and Rorty's prediction about "the breakdown of democratic institutions" is what many claim we are witnessing now with the behavior and decision-making of the GOP. Rorty comes across as a defender of neoliberal capitalism—neoliberalism for short—when he suggests that prior to the "dark years" we had a strong "sense of the relation between the moral order and the economic order."[4] Some philosophers and political commentators disagree with the notion that late twentieth-century and early twenty-first-century capitalism maintained some relationship with morality.[5]

Rorty, however, reflects upon the "apparent incompatibility of capitalism and democracy."[6] For Rorty, one of the causes of the "dark years" is that capitalism finally triumphs over democracy—we might say, after 2016, that capitalism *trumps* democracy. Americans gave up on the democratic project. The wealthy gave up on democracy because it no longer fit their self-interests, and the lower classes—including the middle class—gave up on democracy because of distrust toward government and the "steady breakdown of fraternity" among citizens. This strengthens the claim, in chapter 1, that Rorty changes Plato's pattern: democracy does not turn into tyranny but, rather, American democracy has led to an oligarchy of the

---

3. Rorty, *PSH*, 243.

4. Rorty, *PSH*, 243. This becomes the primary basis for my critique of Rorty's political philosophy.

5. For one example among many, but an important one because he is Rorty's most famous student, see West's "Goodbye, American Neo-Liberalism."

6. Rorty, *PSH*, 244.

"international superrich." Throughout his predictions, Rorty never suggests a deterministic cyclical pattern of government and politics.

This leads to another prediction—which describes exactly where we find ourselves in relation to firearms but not quite where we find ourselves economically:

> [No one] thought that it might be dangerous to make automatic weapons freely and cheaply available to desperate men and women—*people without hope*—living next to the centres of transportation and communication. Those weapons burst into the streets in 2014, in the revolution that, leaving the cities in ruins and dislocating American economic life, plunged the country into the Second Great Depression.[7]

Rorty's prediction about the proliferation of automatic weapons has come to be social reality. In essence, Rorty predicts the mass shootings currently plaguing American social life.

According to the Stanford University MSA Data Project, a mass shooting ought to be defined as "three or more shooting victims (not necessarily fatalities), not including the shooter. The shooting must not be identifiably gang-, drug-, or organized crime–related."[8] Based on this definition, in 2019 alone (only one of the years fitting between 2014 and 2020), three hundred seventy mass shootings occurred, injuring over one thousand people and killing at least four hundred. The difference between a mass shooting and mass murder is how many people die. Rorty does not predict mass murders to increase, only mass shootings. According to Rorty, we should currently think of ourselves in a "revolution" because of gun violence—a revolution, some might say, endorsed and funded by the NRA.

Yet, we do not find ourselves in the Second Great Depression. Rorty wrote this piece in 1996, and he died in 2007. Since 2014, the economy has not only recovered from the 2008 recession but seems to be flourishing. Democrats credit President Obama and his policies for this flourishing; Republicans credit President Trump and his business-mindedness for this flourishing. This seems to be one of the few predictions Rorty is wrong about in our specific time period (2014–2020). From the paragraph quoted above, I conclude: Rorty is right about the gun violence but wrong about the economy.

7. Rorty, *PSH*, 247–48; emphasis added.

8. Stanford Mass Shootings in America, courtesy of the Stanford Geospatial Center and Stanford Libraries: https://library.stanford.edu/projects/mass-shootings-america.

The Dark Years from 2020–2044

In the next paragraph of "Looking Backwards from the Year 2096," Rorty's prediction ought to strike readers as horrible and terrifying. From the years from 2020 to 2044, Rorty predicts:

> The insurgency in the ghettos, coming at a time when all but the wealthiest Americans felt desperately insecure, led to the collapse of [any] trust in government. The collapse of the economy produced a war of all [Americans] against all [Americans], as gasoline and food became harder and harder to buy, and as even the suburbanites began to brandish guns at their neighbors.[9]

Since Rorty was right about the election of a "strongman" in his book *Achieving Our Country*, it becomes horrible and terrifying to think Rorty could be right about the eventual results of that election combined with the economic distance between the wealthiest of the wealthy and everyone else.

While we are not currently in the "Second Great Depression," the assumption that firearms and guns are the solution to our economic and psychological problems has become widespread. Even though we averaged a mass shooting a day in 2019 and even though police officers seem to favor handling African-American men primarily with the power of their weapons, I say that *we are far away from the prediction of "a war of all against all" in this country.*

If food and gasoline become "harder to buy," however, then perhaps we will inch closer to seeing this particular prediction come true. Interestingly, both conservatives and liberals warn that Trump's tariffs will make products like food and gasoline "harder to buy." We learn later that—according to Rorty—the solution to brandishing "guns at their neighbors" becomes solidarity and sympathy. However, we are not quite there yet—neither in terms of Rorty's predictions nor in our current society.

Another prediction Rorty makes about American life in the "dark years" concerns how and why America does not fall into complete annihilation and chaos. Rorty writes, "As the generals never stopped saying throughout the Dark Years, only the military saved the country from utter chaos."[10] The military becomes a type of police force, responding to domestic or internal problems rather than fulfilling its usual role of responding to problems abroad or externally. The strangeness of this claim concerns

9. Rorty, *PSH*, 248.
10. Rorty, *PSH*, 248.

how Rorty puts it: "as the Generals never tire of saying." This suggests a hierarchy of intelligence and order within the "dark years": "the generals" see themselves and their military as the sustainer—perhaps the exclusive sustainer—of American political and social life. Neither the courts,[11] nor the police force,[12] nor citizens rising up in peaceful protests sustain social life:[13] without the military as an internal police force, Americans would annihilate one another during the "dark years."

Rorty predicts that, eventually, even the military will be brought down. Rorty says that in 2044 a "coalition of trade unions and churches" will "topple . . . the military" and "retain . . . control of Congress by specifically convincing the voters that its opponents constitute 'the parties of selfishness.'"[14] This coalition marks the end of the "dark years," politically, but Rorty seems to put his faith more in a process of re-enchantment of shame into sympathy—which I describe in the next chapter—than he does in this coalition for bringing the "dark years" to an end.[15]

Lingering Questions about the Dark Years

Rorty leaves his readers with several questions about the "dark years." Does he envision another American Civil War?[16] Are the wealthy in their bun-

11. Significantly, since his presidential campaign, President Trump has questioned the legitimacy of the courts in the US (see "In His Own Words: The President's Attacks on the Courts").

12. A reasonable inference from Rorty's predictions seems to be that the actual police forces, throughout the United States, become so corrupt and unreliable that they are replaced by military personnel—either deliberately so or *de facto*.

13. Perhaps one way to avoid the "dark years" altogether is to follow the wisdom of Henry David Thoreau's "On Civil Disobedience"—which, although often neglected by readers and scholars of the essay, comes to the following strong conclusion: civil disobedience ought to be allowable among citizens; however, citizens who practice civil disobedience also maintain an obligation—not to "the State" as it is, but to imagine "the State" as it should be.

14. Rorty, *PSH*, 249.

15. Richard Bernstein overstates Rorty's predictions when he claims that the "Democratic Vistas Party" completely settle the "dark years": "In Rorty's imaginary scenario a military dictatorship takes over in 2014 and is finally toppled by the 'Democratic Vistas Party' in 2044" (Bernstein, "Richard Rorty: The Dark Years").

16. Through personal correspondence, presidential historian David Nichols points out that Rorty *must* envision another American Civil War because it would be odd to call these the darkest years of American history in relation to the darkness represented by the Civil War of the nineteenth century (Nichols, correspondence with the author, March 27, 2019).

kers, which we know that they have, the whole time or part of the time or only occasionally? Do the "dark years" and the Second Great Depression coincide for the whole time; in other words, does the fact that we are not currently in a Second Great Depression mean that Rorty has this part of his prediction wrong, or that we still might end up in a Great Depression at some point during the "dark years"?

What is the connection, if any, between placing blame on the academic Left—in *Achieving Our Country*—and the causes of the "dark years"? What do colleges and universities look like during the "dark years"? Will prisons be more full or less full than they are now, and do they continue their likeness to "Jim Crow"?[17]

Rorty gives no answers to these questions. We have no response but political and social despair to these predictions about the "dark years." The self-described philosopher of hope, Richard Rorty, leads us to despair and hopelessness.[18]

---

17. See Alexander's *The New Jim Crow*.

18. I establish what makes Rorty the philosopher of hope in Goodson, *SM*, ch. 10.

Chapter 3

Predictions about the Not Yet
Life after the Dark Years (circa 2045–2095)

In "Looking Backwards from 2096" (published in *Philosophy and Social Hope*), Richard Rorty thinks the "dark years" finally come to an end in the middle part of the twenty-first century. His prediction ought to surprise readers: we put the "dark years" behind us because we (re)turn to seriously reading novels and Scripture. Novels and Scripture reshape our moral and political imaginations.

The academy brings an end to an objective approach to studying and thinking about politics and, instead, political theory becomes a discipline that nurtures and teaches the college-educated to develop sympathy toward other citizens. Philosophy and political science departments, within colleges and universities, will begin to teach and write in ways that seek to (a) encourage sympathy and (b) improve institutions. Why these two? Because philosophers and political scientists will turn their attention toward those citizens who suffer and who tend to be humiliated by institutions. Instead of teaching and writing from a condition of conformity and a disposition of fear (as discussed in chapter 1), philosophers and political scientists will show concern for the downtrodden, helpless, oppressed, out-of-work, and—yes—the poor.[1]

---

1. From a Rortyean perspective, in life after the "dark years," we will begin to see more books like the one recently published by Professor of Political Science at Boston University Spencer Piston called *Class Attitudes in America: Sympathy for the Poor, Resentment of*

My argument in this chapter focuses on how this return or turn to literary narratives, which forms sympathy among and between American citizens, ought to be considered as Rorty's secular version of a process of re-enchantment. By "enchantment," I mean it somewhat close to what Charles Taylor says in *The Secular Age*: "[t]he enchanted world . . . is the world of . . . moral forces which our ancestors lived in."[2] This process of re-enchantment, which Rorty predicts will happen in the middle part of the twenty-first century (2045–2095), involves the following steps: (1) returning or turning to literary narratives that shape our imagination, (2) this produces a sense of shame, (3) this shame turns into sympathy, and (4) this sympathy impacts the attitudes and thoughts of American citizens.[3] Within Rorty's re-enchanted world, sympathy serves as the "moral force" mentioned in the borrowed definition of "enchantment." The twist that I give to Rorty's predictions about the latter half of the twenty-first century concerns why this process ought to be considered a secular re-enchantment.

LIFE AFTER THE DARK YEARS

Pretending to "look backward," Rorty does not think that the whole of the American twenty-first century—post 2014—will be doom and gloom. First, there is the *how* America escapes the "dark years"; second, there is the *what* life looks like post-"dark years." The *how* concerns what I call or consider Rorty's process of re-enchantment, and the *what* concerns the new moral attitude that comes to define life after the "dark years."

Literature and Scripture

According to the unapologetic secular philosopher Richard Rorty, the "dark years" come to an end because American citizens find inspiration

---

the *Rich, and Political Implications*. Piston makes explicit the reasons why Americans have refused and embraced "sympathy toward the poor" and "resentment toward the rich."

2. Taylor, *A Secular Age*, 26. A certain type of reader might read my chapter as "re-describing" Rorty's political philosophy on the terms of Charles Taylor.

3. In "Looking Backwards from the Year 2096," Rorty writes, "Today [2095–2096], morality is thought of neither as a matter of applying the moral law nor as the acquisition of virtues but as fellow feeling, the ability to sympathize with the plight of others" (Rorty, *PSH*, 249).

and seriously read "Scripture and literature."[4] In particular, Rorty claims, "American political discourse has come to be dominated by quotations from Scripture and literature."[5] This shift represents a move away from the alleged and cold objectivity of "political theorists and social scientists" to biblical narratives and novels.

Scripture teaches us humility, love, and sympathy. Churches come back to life because citizens find the biblical narratives so inspiring, and Christian congregations grow because they teach a social gospel theology: "In the churches, the 'social gospel' theology of the early twentieth century has been rediscovered."[6] Rorty thinks the work of his maternal grandfather "saves" both America and Christianity.

Novels also teach us sympathy, and they form a renewed social hope in American citizens. The public schools focus on "social novels," which describe "our past failures to hang together when we needed to."[7] Part of this process also involves turning away from abstract and formal notions of justice toward "inclination[s] of the heart"—inclinations "that produce a sense of shame at having much when others have little."[8] Turning to Scripture and novels provide the *how* out of the "dark years."

The Process of Re-enchantment

Why call this a process of re-enchantment? What might seem to some readers as an off-the-cuff comment or suggestion about American politics pulling itself out of the "dark years" by seriously reading literature and Scripture is, in my judgment, just the tip of the iceberg. To think through this "much more," however, I need to put Rorty in conversation with other scholars who wish to see a re-enchantment of law and politics—in North America and globally as well.

Rorty differs from these scholars in that he *predicts* such a re-enchantment will happen within the United States—which raises a question about distinguishing between wishing for re-enchantment *now* and thinking in terms of the *future* of re-enchantment as repairing the brokenness and suffering we will experience through the "dark years." The nuance or trick of

4. Rorty, *PSH*, 249.
5. Rorty, *PSH*, 249.
6. Rorty, *PSH*, 249.
7. Rorty, *PSH*, 249.
8. Rorty, *PSH*, 248.

my overall argument concerns how Rorty says that biblical narratives will play a role in the process of re-enchantment, but this does not mean that the process of re-enchantment ought to be considered a Christian or even religious process of re-enchantment. Instead, Rorty offers an argument that leads to a secular version of re-enchantment.[9]

First, Rorty's description of the "dark years" echoes the fully developed thesis found in Bernard Stiegler's *The Re-enchantment of the World: The Value of Spirit Against Industrial Populism*. Stiegler's thesis is: "Only a fight against the stupidity imposed . . . by industrial populism, represents a real possibility of 're-enchanting the world.'"[10] Steigler argues that the mix of late capitalism, political populism, and the rise of "technoscience" have brought us to the point of a shallow and superficial disenchanted world.[11] The problem of late capitalism, according to Stiegler, is that its "very principle . . . rests upon the limitless increase of consumption"—which blinds us to deeper realities and puts us on a "suicidal" path for the whole of humanity.[12] Stiegler thinks that we will shop ourselves to death!

The problem of political populism, according to Stiegler, is that it leads to "stupidity" at the societal level. Stiegler argues that political populism in the twenty-first century contains three features: mental regression, moral debasement, and a spirit-less intelligence. By spirit-less intelligence, Stiegler means that the collective "spirit" of populism is void of intelligence while displays of intelligence that might occur seem to remain only at the level of individuality. There is no collective intelligence evident in the

---

9. What follows is my lengthy response to Ronald A. Kuipers's argument—found in *Solidarity and the Stranger: Themes in the Social Philosophy of Richard Rorty*—that Rorty's "hope" for the world is further disenchantment: Rorty is "deeply concerned about doing justice to the rich, meaningful dimensions of human being-in-the-world, and to the suffering people who announce themselves there, even if this world for him is a thoroughly naturalized, secularized, and disenchanted one" (Kuipers, SS, 104). Kuipers is right about Rorty's secularism, but he is wrong about Rorty being a naturalist and promoting disenchantment. Kuipers confuses enchantment with "Christian metaphysics," a question I address later in this section. I engage more fully with Kuipers's book in chapter 4.

10. Stiegler, *Re-enchantment of the World*, 5.

11. About "technoscience," Stiegler makes two observations: science becomes reduced to the end(s) of technological development, and wealth becomes tied to technological corporations. To be pro-STEM, at the expense of the humanities and liberal arts, correlates with being pro-corporation.

12. See Stiegler, *Re-enchantment of the World*, 4.

twenty-first century. This is why Stiegler so boldly calls our current time the age of "stupidity."[13]

How do Stiegler's arguments relate to Rorty's predictions? The commonality between Rorty and Stiegler involves their diagnosis of populism. Rorty does not use this word much in his writings, but his characterization concerning how and why the US will elect a "strongman" in 2016 can be labeled as the result of populism—namely a large portion of the American population rising up against the academic Left and elitism.[14] Trump is a financial elite who uses anti-elitist rhetoric to fuel the populism that he relies upon for his own popularity and support. The difference between Rorty and Stiegler is the difference between Rorty and the majority of his colleagues in philosophy departments: the priority of rationality and reason. Stiegler thinks re-enchantment will come through the proper use of reason, whereas Rorty emphasizes and promotes the faculty or use of the imagination.

Second, like Rorty, James K. A. Smith posits the role of the imagination within the process of re-enchantment. Smith writes, "To resist . . . requires the imagination to think the world otherwise . . . . Reenchantment requires a kind of theorizing that is imaginative—which is not constrained by the rules and regulations imposed by the 'plausibility structures' of secular modernity."[15] Rorty, of course, is not against "secular modernity" as a whole—indeed he is one of its biggest champions—but, like Smith, Rorty too worries about the "plausibility structures" that are used to *justify* "secular modernity." In "Postmodern Bourgeois Liberalism," for instance, Rorty performs a deconstruction of meta-narratives because we tend to use them as grand theories about human culture, human progress, and human success that we tell ourselves in order to *justify* our institutions and practices. On the one hand, Rorty champions the institutions and progress of liberalism. On the other hand, he thinks liberals make a serious mistake when they play the game of *justifying* their own institutions and progress because such justification always relies on a meta-narrative. Both Rorty and Smith agree on the role of the imagination within the process of re-enchantment, but Smith ties the use of imagination with a substantial Christian metaphysic.

Is it possible to champion the imagination within the process of re-enchantment without tying it to a Christian metaphysic? The quick answer

13. For further reading on this theme, see Stiegler's *States of Shock*, 42–61.

14. See Latner, "'Populism' Is More Accurately 'Anti-Elitism.'"

15. Smith, "Secularity, Globalization, and the Re-enchantment," 11.

to this question is yes, because of the role of power within Christian meta-physics. Christian metaphysics seems necessarily to rely on a hierarchy of being where power becomes prioritized and ranked.[16] The imagination certainly is required for constructing and understanding the hierarchy of being, but it remains difficult to avoid making power dynamics and power-relations static in the hierarchy of being. Part of the reason to emphasize Rorty's process of re-enchantment as secular involves seeking to avoid the role of power within Christian metaphysics.

Significantly, this point relates to one of Rorty's predictions about the Roman Catholic Church: by the 2090s, Rorty predicts that there will be female priests. One of these ordained priest is named Cynthia Rodriguez, SJ, and she serves as the coeditor for the fictional volume where Rorty's chapter is published.[17] For female priesthood to be a real possibility within the Roman Catholic Church, the static hierarchies of being found within Christian metaphysics will have to be challenged if not altogether "de-stroyed"—in Martin Heidegger's sense of the term.[18]

Third, in "The Turn to Imagination in Legal Theory," Mark Antaki casts "doubt on the tendency to tie enchantment to Christian metaphysics, i.e. to the belief in another world that is the ground of this one."[19] Antaki elaborates, "[W]e should resist the contemporary tendency to identify dis-enchantment with the death of the Christian God and hence to equate en-chantment solely . . . with Christian metaphysics."[20] Instead, Antaki argues, "[f]ollowing Nietzsche and Heidegger, one ought to grasp Christianity itself as a set of moments in the history of the disenchantment of the world."[21] An-taki claims that the role of the imagination within re-enchantment should not be undergirded by Christian metaphysics because re-enchantment, itself, can be understood as "the opposite of metaphysics." Antaki articu-lates the process of re-enchantment closest to Rorty's own thinking since Rorty identifies as a post-metaphysical intellectual and public philosopher. To put Antaki's point in Rorty's terms: meta-narratives block the use of the imagination, and metaphysics continues the disenchantment of the world.

16. See Taylor, *A Secular Age*, 25–28.

17. See Rorty, *PSH*, 243.

18. See Heidegger, *Being and Time*, 19–25.

19. Antaki, "Turn to Imagination in Legal Theory," 3.

20. Antaki, "Turn to Imagination in Legal Theory," 4–5.

21. Antaki, "Turn to Imagination in Legal Theory," 5.

Antaki and Rorty differ, however, on where the process of re-enchantment leads in terms of a new moral attitude. For Rorty, this process will result in sympathy. For Antaki, re-enchantment involves empathy. How do these differ in substance and vision?

The New Moral Attitude: Empathy or Sympathy?

According to Antaki, processes of re-enchantment lead to the new moral attitude of empathy within law and politics. Antaki defines empathy "as the making present to oneself . . . the inner lives of others."[22] Antaki turns to the work of Martha Nussbaum in order to think through the relationship between empathy and literature. Antaki lists three quotations from Nussbaum's work that he finds helpful:

> The novel helps to "cultivate the ability to imagine what it is like to live the life of another person who might, given changes in circumstances, be oneself or one of one's loved ones."[23]

> "[T]he novel, as a genre, in its basic structure and aspiration, is . . . a defender of the Enlightenment ideal of the equality and dignity of all human life . . . ."[24]

> Literature, particularly certain literary forms such as the "realist Anglo-American novel," is invaluable in [the] cultivation [of empathy].[25]

Antaki takes from these Nussbaumian insights what he calls a "progressive legal imagination"—which seeks inspiration and wisdom from literature, in order to "conceive of law as an instrument of world-improvement."[26] By "world-improvement," Antaki means achieving "goals such as greater equality and respect for human rights."[27] The inspiration and wisdom that come from literature concerns how "empathy is closely tied to the narrative

22. Antaki, "Turn to Imagination in Legal Theory," 9.

23. Antaki, "Turn to Imagination in Legal Theory," 9; see Nussbaum, *Poetic Justice*, 5.

24. Antaki, "Turn to Imagination in Legal Theory," 9; see Nussbaum, *Poetic Justice*, 46.

25. Antaki, "Turn to Imagination in Legal Theory," 9; see Nussbaum, *Poetic Justice*, 10.

26. Antaki, "Turn to Imagination in Legal Theory," 9.

27. Antaki, "Turn to Imagination in Legal Theory," 9.

choices made by advocates and serves as a corrective to narrow understand-ings of rationality and of the rule-bound character of legal judgment[s]."[28] Literature broadens the narrowness of legal reasoning, and literature serves "to cultivate the capacity of imagination so crucial to progressive lawyering and judging."[29]

This empathy becomes part and parcel of a re-enchanted world be-cause, still following Nussbaum, it acknowledges the ancient category of tragedy within our everyday lives. Empathy helps us better understand the tragic nature of life, and tragedy in turn requires us to strengthen our ap-preciation for "universal human dignity." Antaki thinks that the category of tragedy tunes us into an enchanted world, and he thinks that empathy makes us better listeners in relation to those who are disenfranchised.

Rorty might agree with much of this,[30] but Rorty remains skeptical about the potential to be empathic. Empathy involves an epistemological claim about knowing "the inner lives of others," a problem that falls under Rorty's career-long critiques of representationalism. In addition to this epistemological problem, empathy also seems like a version of secular self-righteousness—in the sense that one claims that he/she can truly appreciate and understand the plight and suffering of strangers. Rorty gets around these problems by calling for sympathy, not empathy.

A longtime colleague and friend of Rorty, Richard Bernstein (profes-sor of Philosophy at the New School for Social Research in New York City), describes Rorty's call for sympathy in the terms of its connection with the power of journalism and novels. About Rorty's political philosophy, Bern-stein writes:

> Powerful novels (like Charles Dickens') and muckraking jour-nalism (like Upton Sinclair's) are far more effective in getting people to do something about horrendous social injustices than the academic tracts of philosophers and those infatuated with "theorizing" . . . . So instead of better and more sophisticated lib-eral and democratic *theory*, the right sorts of novels, muckraking

28. Antaki, "Turn to Imagination in Legal Theory," 9.

29. Antaki, "Turn to Imagination in Legal Theory," 9.

30. Rorty explicitly states the following agreements with Nussbaum: "I heartily agree with Nussbaum that 'there are valuable aspects of human moral experience that are not tapped by traditional books of moral philosophy' . . . , and I agree that 'a philosophical book would have a hard time mounting a direct argument' for the claim that 'infidelity and failure of response are more or less inevitable features even of the best examples of loving'" (Rorty, "Redemption from Egotism," 399).

> journalism, and op-ed articles may accomplish more to strengthen and improve liberal institutions than endless academic tracts of political philosophers. This fits in with another of Rorty's deepest convictions. Liberal societies depend on a sense of solidarity with and sympathy for one's fellow human beings. It makes little sense to speak about universal sympathy, for this is frequently quite empty. Moral and liberal progress involves enlarging our sense of sympathy for suffering human beings and those who are institutionally humiliated. This is accomplished by the literary skills of novelists and the reporting skills of journalists who are able to arouse our sense of *injustice*, our indignation at outrageous forms of humiliation . . . . Moral progress comes about when our sense of solidarity, our sympathy with those who are institutionally humiliated, is extended and deepened.[31]

According to Bernstein, journalism and novels are the genres that increase the amount of sympathy.

While empathy involves the knowledge of "the inner lives of others," sympathy relates to decreasing the amount of humiliation—especially that of those who experience humiliation at the hands of institutions. According to Bernstein, Rorty does not envision—I would say predict—"universal sympathy." I think Bernstein is right about this, which provides another contrast from Antaki's plea for empathy in relation to "universal human dignity."

However, one of Rorty's main defenders—William M. Curtis, professor of Political Science at the University of Portland—argues that Rorty indeed defends *empathy*.[32] Curtis writes, "It is empathy, induced by . . . our imaginative capacities, our ability to 'put ourselves into the shoes of Others' and see them as fellow sufferers, that is the first step toward accepting them as . . . equals and extending formal justice to them."[33] Curtis concludes

31. Bernstein, "Rorty's Inspirational Liberalism," 131–32.

32. Steven A. Miller comes to this conclusion as well but provides neither a defense of nor explanation for it: "Human solidarity is made rather than found. We must hope that we can find ways to create the conditions necessary to make it [solidarity] a reality . . . . Rorty, then, recognize[s] that at present we are unable to find the universal moral community. It is only through more work—empathetic [work] for Rorty—that we may be able to find or make such a community for ourselves" (Miller, *Community and Loyalty*, 88). For my engagement with Miller's interpretation of Rorty's use of "solidarity," see the next chapter. For my judgments on Miller's book as a whole, see my review of Miller's *Community and Loyalty* in the *American Journal of Theology and Philosophy* (forthcoming).

33. Curtis, *Defending Rorty*, 92.

his section on empathy by noting that Rorty "joins Martha Nussbaum in his contention that narrative is more important for moral and political progress than [any] theory is."[34] According to Curtis, Rorty thinks the turn to literary narratives will lead citizens to cultivate empathy. These claims misinterpret Rorty's moral reasoning and political philosophy, and I utilize these misinterpretations to draw my own conclusions about Rorty's understanding of shame and sympathy.

RORTY'S SECULAR PROCESS OF RE-ENCHANTMENT

I appreciate Bernstein's and Curtis's interpretations of Rorty's political philosophy because both help me clarify my own interpretation of Rorty's predictions about the latter half of the twenty-first century.

As a conclusion to this chapter as well as to Part 1, I clarify my interpretation of Rorty concerning the process of re-enchantment as American life will shift out of the "dark years" approximately twenty-five years from now.

a. In relation to both Bernstein's and Curtis's interpretations, I read Rorty as making predictions about what America will be like but only after we experience or go through thirty years of darkness (the "dark years")—not as spelling out, in a seemingly top-down theoretical way, what Rorty seeks for America.

b. In relation to both Bernstein's and Curtis's interpretations, I read Rorty as saying that our moral attitudes will change as a result of a process of re-enchantment where novels and Scripture—in short, literary narratives—re-shape our attitudes and thinking over time.

c. In relation to Curtis's interpretation, I think the difference between Nussbaum's and Rorty's social visions comes down to a difference between *empathy* and *sympathy*: Antaki's interpretation of Nussbaum strikes me as the correct one of her work whereas Curtis's interpretation of Rorty seems to me too representationalist in the sense that Rorty thinks we can neither have knowledge of "the inner lives of others" nor "put ourselves into the shoes of Others."

d. In relation to Curtis's interpretation, I think Rorty avoids and disavows any attempt to extend "formal justice" to anyone—not out of a

34. Curtis, *Defending Rorty*, 92–93.

lack of sympathy for individuals who suffer injustices; rather, "formal justice" repeats the mistakes of political science identified by Rorty in "Looking Backwards from 2096": after 2045 or so, political and social scientists are no longer helpful because they continue to "formulate principles of justice, equality, and liberty, and invoke these principles when weighing hard moral or legal issues," but the citizens no longer care because they have become shaped by the narratives of literature and Scripture in such a way "that produces a sense of shame at having much when others have little."[35]

In my judgment, and what other interpreters of Rorty's political philosophy seem uniformly to miss, this production of "a sense of shame" involves two directions relating to Rorty's prediction about the process of re-enchantment twenty-five years from now (2045): turning to literary narratives led American citizens to develop this "sense of shame," and this "sense of shame" transforms into a sense of sympathy.[36] From Rorty's perspective, this marks the difference between our own time of entering the "dark years" and American life after such darkness: both now and twenty-five years from now involve shame, but *the "dark years" are based upon a shame transformed into a politics of fear whereas life after the "dark years" will be a time when shame is transformed into sympathy.* Although Rorty does not use the words enchanted or enchantment, this transformation of shame into sympathy only makes sense in terms of re-enchantment because the best (perhaps the only) way to understand how we exit the "dark years" involves a type of *magical transformation* of shame into sympathy—instead of the more customary or usual transformation of shame into fear.

A FINAL PREDICTION

Rorty's final prediction concerns international politics. Rorty predicts America's role at the international level, from 2045–2095, will look like this: "Compared with the Americans of 100 years ago, we are citizens of an isolationist, unambitious, middle-grade nation."[37] In America's place stands

> the European community, which was able to withstand the pressures of a globalized labor market by having a fully fledged welfare

---

35. Rorty, *PSH*, 248.
36. I continue down this path in the next chapter.
37. Rorty, *PSH*, 250.

state already in place, and which (except for . . . Great Britain) was able to resist the temptation to impoverish the most vulnerable in order to keep its suburbanites affluent. Spared the equivalent of our own Dark Years, Europe . . . holds the position we lost in 2014: it still dominates both the world's economy and its culture.[38]

Rorty mentions that China comes a close second to Europe in terms of being dominant in relation to "the world's economy and . . . culture."[39]

While he does not mention Brexit, the parenthetical comment suggests that Great Britain differs from the "European community" in some significant way. Does this parenthetical remark mean that, since he predicted the rise of populism in the United States, he predicted the rise of populism in the United Kingdom?

In a statement made by Rorty right before his death, he offers a terse summary of his own global "social hope." In a German publication, Rorty comments to a journalist:

[The hope is] that people in the future will enjoy more money, more freedom, more social equality and that they might develop more imagination . . . , more sympathy, so that they may be in a better position to transform themselves into other people. The hope is that people will become more decent as the material circumstances of their lives improve.[40]

Now on to the assessment of what Rorty means by "more imagination," "more sympathy," and—most of all—social hope.

38. Rorty, *PSH*, 250.

39. Rorty, *PSH*, 250.

40. Quoted by Schneewind, "Rorty on Utopia," 489.

PART 2

The Philosophy of Hope

FROM HERE, THE ARGUMENT of the book goes in two different yet related directions. First, I explain Rorty's social hope—which is shorthand for his political philosophy—but strongly critique the ways in which a type of neoliberalism maintains a residue on Rorty's political and social vision. Second, Rorty's social hope is mistaken for both spatial and temporal reasons: spatially, we need an account of hope that refuses to be monopolized by politics; temporally, our hopes do not need to be projected so far into the future. Rather, we can enjoy and experience the best parts of Rorty's social hope sooner rather than later.

In chapter 4, continuing the argument of chapter 3, I focus on what Rorty means by solidarity and sympathy in relation to the role of reading literature and novels. While I defend his understanding of the role of reading literature and novels, I critique or question his account of solidarity and sympathy because they contain a residue of neoliberalism. By neoliberalism, I mean the tendency to re-define "citizens as 'customers' or 'clients'" where institutions think of themselves in terms of cultivating "an 'entrepreneurial spirit'" rather than promoting the common good.[1] Neoliberalism will further be defined and described as needed throughout the book.

1. See Steger and Roy, *Neoliberalism*, 13. In addition to Steger and Roy, my understanding of neoliberalism has been shaped deeply by Kotsko's *Neoliberalism's Demons*.

Chapter 5 provides my explanation of Rorty's philosophy of religion—especially how it contributes and relates to his philosophy of hope. Whereas chapter 4 explores the concepts of solidarity and sympathy, chapter 5 focuses on the concepts of charity and love. While chapter 4 explores the role of reading literature and novels, chapter 5 focuses on the role of reading Scripture. Specifically, I focus on his turn toward 1 Corinthians 13.

Chapter 4

Social Hope, Solidarity, and Sympathy
The Work of Novels

BEGINNING AROUND 2045, RORTY envisions a magical transformation from the "dark years" to a time defined and determined by love, solidarity, and sympathy. Charity and love are the focus of chapter 5; solidarity and sympathy receive attention in this chapter.

Rorty borrows from yet tweaks J. S. Mill's moral reasoning in his theory of justice.[1] For Mill, vengefulness leads to sympathy; sympathy results in systemic justice. For Rorty, shame leads to sympathy; yet, sympathy does not lead to systemic justice but results in what Rorty calls solidarity. However, in a 1997 essay, Rorty puts himself closer to Mill's moral reasoning by seemingly equating his use of solidarity with justice—a suggestion found in Steven A. Miller's *Community and Loyalty in American Philosophy* (2018).

In addition to solidarity and sympathy, this chapter concerns the themes of friendship, justice, neighbors, strangers, and the work of novels. The chapter proceeds as follows. First, I borrow from Dianne Rothleder's *The Work of Friendship* (1999) to outline what Rorty envisions as the work of novels. Second, I engage with Ronald Kuipers's *Solidarity and the Stranger* (1997) to substantiate my own development of the difference between neighbors and strangers within Rorty's accounts of solidarity and

---

1. I disagree with J. B. Schneewind that Rorty's political philosophy merely repeats Mill's political philosophy: "Rorty has not gotten us beyond Mill" (Schneewind, "Rorty on Utopia," 493).

sympathy. Third, as previously stated, I build from Steven A. Miller's suggestion concerning the interchangeability between justice and solidarity within Rorty's writings. Fourth, I return to Rothleder's *The Work of Friendship* in order to mount a full critique of Rorty's accounts of justice, solidarity, and sympathy. Rothleder introduces the ways in which the category of friendship serves us better than Rorty's defenses of solidarity and sympathy do. Fifth, and finally, I engage with Todd May's *Friendship in an Age of Economics* (2012) as a way to say more about friendship in relationship to neoliberalism—neoliberalism having family resemblances with Rorty's accounts of justice, solidarity, and sympathy—and why the categories of fraternity and friendship ought to become our social hope in addition to solidarity and sympathy.

THE MAGICAL TRANSFORMATION OF SHAME INTO SYMPATHY

In chapter 3, I argued that the best (and perhaps only) way to understand how we exit the "dark years" involves a type of *magical transformation of shame into sympathy*. What does this magical transformation look like? I answer this question in two ways: (a) demonstrating the magical transformation of shame into sympathy, through reading novels, involves the *work* of novels and (b) outlining what Rorty, himself, recommends in terms of which novelists to read for this transformation and what sympathy will look like from 2045–2095.

The Work of Novels

What is the *work* of novels? In her book on Rorty's philosophy, Dianne Rothleder gives us seven ways to answer this question. For clarity's sake, I outline all seven ways.

First, "Rorty . . . argues that novels and narratives are important sources of information" because of "the effect that stories have on readers";[2]

---

2. Rothleder, *WF*, 3. In this passage, Rothleder claims that reading novels ought to lead to "empathy" but recognizes that Rorty's critique of representationalism—as I stated in the previous chapter—does not allow for empathy, only for sympathy. Rothleder critiques Rorty for not allowing for empathy, whereas I am embracing sympathy over empathy in my own argument. Unlike Curtis and Miller, however, Rothleder does not make the mistake of asserting that Rorty defends empathy instead of sympathy.

this "effect" involves how novels speak the unspeakable, and Rorty's "unspeakable" concerns the "shame and fear" that we live with both privately and publicly.[3]

Second, novels introduce readers to new vocabularies. In Rothleder's words, "novels . . . move us smoothly from one vocabulary to another, from a re-description to a re-redescription."[4] Rorty uses the word "re-description" in order to articulate the significance of taking on various descriptions about one's self. By being introduced to new vocabularies through reading novels, readers gain more descriptions of themselves.

Third, novels begin with what is familiar to readers and then introduce new and unfamiliar vocabularies. In essence, this third answer responds to a question lingering from the second answer: why should readers trust the new vocabularies found within novels? The new vocabularies become trustworthy because novels begin with what is familiar to readers, or—better put—readers treat novels on the terms of familiarity and then allow novels to introduce new vocabularies to them. Rothleder describes the process on these terms: "novels . . . start with what is most familiar, what makes us feel for a time that we are inside the novel."[5] She continues, "Through measured steps, a novel . . . take[s] us to less familiar terrain, but only by putting the new in the vocabulary of the familiar, only by inviting in."[6] She claims that novels seduce "us with a heady mixture of the exotic and the unknown," which means they continually tempt "us to turn pages."[7]

Fourth, in order to strike the balance required in the previous answer, "novels must . . . be real accounts of fictional people. That is, novels are bound by convention, by the desire to be read and consumed, to stay within familiar terrain."[8] The characters within novels are relatable to their readers, and this relatability means that readers become open to transformation on the terms of the characters.

The fifth answer that Rothleder provides to the question "What is the *work* of novels for Rorty?" involves the relationship between the "familiar" and the "real." She writes: "[F]amiliarity takes the place of the

3. Rothleder, *WF*, 4.

4. Rothleder, *WF*, 20.

5. Rothleder, *WF*, 20.

6. Rothleder, *WF*, 20–21.

7. Rothleder, *WF*, 21.

8. Rothleder, *WF*, 21.

real" in the sense that "it is not the 'real' world that novels represent, but only the 'familiar' world."[9]

Sixth, novels help readers live in the tension between comfort and being challenged by difference or otherness. On Rothleder's terms: "[W]e . . . comfortably enter into the 'novel' [and] discover a crucial difference, but we are comforted by the basic familiarity of the situation."[10] The "familiar," as found within novels, helps readers negotiate the tensions—tensions that they will experience within their everyday lives—between being challenged and remaining comfortable.

The seventh and final answer concerns the only moral obligation found within Rorty's philosophy. The only moral obligation Rorty gives to American citizens is "to read lots and lots of books, especially novels, in which characters are humiliated so that she [the American citizen] can learn what humiliates and hence what kinds of public discourse she must avoid."[11] US citizens have a moral obligation to read as many novels as possible, and reading novels will lead to a deeper awareness of how others experience and face humiliation. Another word for this awareness of humiliation is shame, and this shame will magically transform into sympathy. What we have learned is that this magical transformation involves seeing people in the world on the terms of characters in novels—which leads to recognizing humiliation within the world, and this recognition leads to sympathy toward others.[12]

I agree with these seven ways concerning why Rorty thinks reading novels are transformative, but two caveats to my agreement become important for the interpretation of Rorty's philosophy developed in this book: this transformation ought to be understood as part of Rorty's secular version of the process of re-enchantment because it remains mostly magical that our shame does not disappear but leads to sympathy rather

---

9. Rothleder, *WF*, 21.

10. Rothleder, *WF*, 23–24.

11. Rothleder, *WF*, 65.

12. Through personal correspondence, Diane Rothleder claims that she is not as hopeful about the work of novels as I present her arguments to be; she writes, "I don't think we can really count on novels unless the word 'novel' is shorthand for story, and story is shorthand for all the encounters we have. As I recall, in the book I come down on the side of reading as insufficient, as calling more for actual social relations, while recognizing some of the problems we run into because we experience different worlds even while standing in the same room or walking on the same street" (Rothleder, correspondence with the author, June 16, 2019).

than to fear; this transformation will take place, for Rorty, only after a thirty-year period of darkness.[13]

Imaginative Literature, Intellectual Autonomy, and Intense Reading

Rorty revisits his claim about the significance of literature and novels in an essay entitled "Redemption from Egotism." Originally published in Spanish, "Redemption from Egotism" came out in 2001.[14] In this essay, Rorty follows the recommendations of Yale professor Harold Bloom concerning what American citizens should read in the twenty-first century.

He (Rorty) argues "imaginative literature," not argumentative literature (think philosophy, political science, religious studies, sociology, theology), leads readers to what can be considered intellectual autonomy. Intellectual autonomy is a type of autonomy that helps us recognize the ways in which we remain trapped in our own prejudices and stereotypes in relation to how we think about other human beings—particularly those who differ in their identities.[15] I call these people—those who differ in their identities—*strangers* throughout this chapter. Rorty suggests that our prejudices and stereotypes about other human beings lead to us buckling down more in terms of our own egos, greed, and selfishness. Imaginative literature offers redemption from that buckling down. Although this essay does not explicitly make predictions, Rorty's tone seems to project an account of sympathy into a later period of American life. Also, we learn that part of what Rorty means by sympathy includes individuals finding redemption in relation to their own egotism, greed, and selfishness. This redemption and sympathy only come about through what Rorty calls "constant and intense

---

13. On the one hand, Ronald Kuipers argues that Rorty promotes a disenchanted world. On the other hand, Kuipers admits that Rorty thinks of literature as a mysterious "mechanism . . . through which such progress is effected": Rorty "sees literature playing a key role in helping us reconcile the existing tension between private and public concerns"—that is, "he claims that literature helps us look up from our private concerns and notice others" (Kuipers, SS, 74). This mechanism is mysterious in the sense that Rorty "does not think there is anything, including literature, that can provide a metaphysical guarantee that we will all get it together" (Kuipers, SS, 75).

14. Citations refer to the version published in *The Rorty Reader*: Rorty, RE, ch. 23.

15. Rorty writes: "[I]maginative novelty, rather than argumentation . . . , does most for the autonomy of the entranced reader"—this "kind of autonomy . . . is . . . the sort that liberates one from one's previous ways of thinking about the lives and fortunes of other human beings" (Rorty, RE, 389–90).

reading."[16] For clarity's sake, I outline the six pertinent points from Rorty's "Redemption from Egotism."

First, reading novels leads to the cultivation of sympathy in their readers. How so?

> It is by causing us to rethink our judgments of particular people that imaginative literature does most to help us break with our own pasts. The resulting liberation may, of course, lead one to try to change the political or economic . . . status quo. Such an attempt may begin a lifetime of effort to break through the received ideas that serve to justify present-day institutions. But it also may result merely in one's becoming a more sensitive, more knowledgable, wiser person. The latter is the sort of change that comes over Lambert Strether (the hero of [Henry] James's novel *The Ambassadors*). This sort of change—increase of sympathy rather than change of ideas—contrasts with the sort of change that comes over Tom Joad (the hero of Steinbeck's *The Grapes of Wrath*), and also with the sort described in novels that focus on loss or acquisition of religious faith.[17]

Right away, we have recommendations by Rorty for which authors—and their particular novels—to read: Henry James's *The Ambassadors* (1903) and George Steinbeck's *The Grapes of Wrath* (1939).[18] These two novels do not lead their readers to sympathy in identical ways, but both of them help form sympathy in readers. More general recommendations from Rorty involve "novels that focus on loss or acquisition of religious faith," and one that comes to mind for me is Barbara Kingsolver's *The Poisonwood Bible* (1998).

Second, although journalism remains important, novels become and remain more helpful. Rorty argues,

16. Rorty writes: "I want now to narrow my focus from imaginative literature to the novel—the genre that Henry James rightly called 'the most independent, the most elastic, the most prodigious of literary forms'. The novel is the best illustration of [how redemption and sympathy] results [from] constant and intense reading" (Rorty, RE, 392).

17. Rorty, RE, 390.

18. About *The Grapes of Wrath*, Rorty writes elsewhere: "Perhaps the most vivid description of the American concept of fraternity is found in a passage from John Steinbeck's 1939 novel *The Grapes of Wrath*. Steinbeck describes a desparately impoverished family, dispossessed tenant farmers from Oklahoma, camped out at the edge of Highway 66, sharing their food with an even more desperate immigrant family. Steinbeck writes: "'I have a little food' plus 'I have none'. If from this problem, the sum is 'We have little food', the movement has direction." As long as people in trouble can sacrifice to help people who are in still worse trouble, Steinbeck insisted, there is fraternity, and therefore social hope" (Rorty, PSH, 248).

> In our own time . . . , journalism continue[s] to broaden our sense
> of the possibilities open to human lives. But the novel is the genre
> which gives us most help in grasping the variety of human life and
> the contingency of our own moral vocabulary.[19]

Novels stretch our imaginations, and this stretching helps us recognize the
limitations of our own perspective and the various ways of life all around us.

Third, novels teach us sympathy toward religious believers and politicians we despise. Rorty reasons,

> Novels are the principal means which help us imagine what it is
> like to be a cradle Catholic losing his faith, a redneck fundamen-
> talist taking Jesus into her heart . . . , or an idealistic politician
> coping with the pressures that multinational corporations bring to
> bear on the political process.[20]

While some might not like certain religious believers, reading novels about
religious believers will lead to having some sympathy for them. Rorty's religious examples here concern two types of Christians: someone raised as
a Roman Catholic who no longer participates within the life of the church,
and someone not raised as a Christian yet who converts to Christianity
and becomes an American Evangelical Christian. If one has no sympathy
toward American Evangelical Christians or lapsed Roman Catholics, then
reading novels about these types of Christians will help one become sympathetic toward them.

Rorty's political example is an "idealistic politician" who cannot shake
the power of corporations and their lobbyists. If one has no sympathy toward such a politician—and, presumably, if one lacks sympathy toward
lobbyists as well—then reading novels about politicians (and lobbyists) will
help one become more sympathetic toward them. A novel that comes to
mind for me is Christopher Buckley's *Thank You for Smoking* (1994).

Fourth, those who read novels seek redemption from their previous
unsympathetic judgments about others. Rorty writes, "Novel-readers . . .
are seeking redemption from insensitivity rather than from [their own] im-
piety or irrationality."[21] This is Rorty's way to contrast his view concerning
the type of morality shaped by reading novels from the more traditional
views that reading literary narratives make readers more perfect, pious,

19. Rorty, RE, 393.
20. Rorty, RE, 394.
21. Rorty, RE, 395.

rational, and/or virtuous.[22] For Rorty, reading novels leads to less insensitivity and more sympathy; in "Redemption from Egotism," Rorty defends neither moral nor rational perfectionism.[23]

Where should one begin in terms of reading novels that lead to more sympathy? Fifth, Rorty recommends beginning with Henry James's novels: "[Henry] James is good at showing us what it is like to notice things about other people—their needs, their fears, their self-descriptions, their descriptions of other people—which we are usually too egoistic to take account of."[24] James, himself, hinted at this when he claimed that reading novels is "the very record and mirror of the general adventure of one's intelligence."[25] How do James's novels achieve this? Because, according to Rorty, he "creates a character with a set of self-descriptions and a moral outlook that we had never before imagined."[26]

Sixth, and lastly, sympathy represents an addition—not a subtraction. Rorty writes, "Novel-reading . . . aims at encompassing multitudes rather than eliminating superfluities."[27] The kind of sympathy gained through reading novels is not one that requires a type of conversion experience where an individual must give up some aspect of him or herself in order to become legitimately and properly sympathetic. Rather, sympathy ought to be understood as an addition to one's character and identity—adding to who one already is.[28]

Ronald Kuipers claims two novelists as the best to read in order to fulfill Rorty's expectations: Vladimir Nabokov and George Orwell. Both novelists, according to Kuipers, "awaken us from our metaphysical slumber and [help] focus our cultural energy on solving the particular injustices of

---

22. We might contrast Rorty's proposal with those made by Stanley Hauerwas (reading novels helps Christians become more pious), Alasdair MacIntyre (reading novels—particularly Jane Austen—makes readers more virtuous), Iris Murdoch (reading novels helps readers in relation to moral perfectionism), and Martha Nussbaum (reading novels leads to more rationality).

23. In *SM*, I use arguments from Rorty's *Philosophy and Social Hope* to put his thinking in the tradition of rational perfectionism.

24. Rorty, RE, 399.

25. Quoted by Rorty, RE, 399.

26. Rorty, RE, 403.

27. Rorty, RE, 406.

28. Rorty's point goes along with my defense and explanation of the process of mentoring in Goodson, *SM*, ch. 4.

our own time and place."[29] Rorty has essays on both Nabokov and Orwell in *Contingency, Irony, and Solidarity*, and Kuipers interprets Rorty's use of these novelists with some pessimism: "[U]nfortunately, there is no guarantee that everyone is going to read Vladimir Nabokov or George Orwell . . . and learn the lessons embodied in their great stories."[30] Kuipers seems to confuse Rorty's point in recommending novels: Rorty's claim—and the claim of the present chapter—is not that everyone will begin reading novels around the year 2045 but, rather, that *enough citizens will have their shame transformed into sympathy* (instead of fear) *by reading novels that eventually it will make a difference at political and social levels.*

In *Strength of Mind*, I recommend Ray Bradbury's *Fahrenheit 451* and Herman Melville's *Moby Dick* for helping undergraduate students know the right questions to ask of and about themselves.[31] In addition to knowing the right questions to ask about one's self, I think that both novels lead to sympathy in their readers. In finding redemption from our egotism, greed, and selfishness, we cultivate sympathy for the stranger. However, the final judgment I make on Rorty's account of redemption is that it fails because it does not speak to our friendships and personal relationships. The reason for this limitation is that Rorty's political philosophy maintains the residue of neoliberalism, and his defense of redemption does not provide an exception to this rule but falls right back into Rorty's neoliberalism. I defend these claims throughout the remainder of the book, and readers can go to the Conclusion for an account of redemption that avoids neoliberalism.

THE MAGICAL TRANSFORMATION OF CRUELTY INTO SOLIDARITY

Although Rorty's predictions explicitly state that shame will transform into sympathy during life after the "dark years," on my interpretation of his political philosophy this process of re-enchantment also includes the magical transformation of cruelty into solidarity. According to Rorty, cruelty is the only sin. Our social hope becomes the culmination of cultivating sympathy toward strangers and developing solidarity with neighbors. My claim is

29. Kuipers, *SS*, 76.

30. Kuipers, *SS*, 76.

31. See Goodson, *SM*, ch. 10.

that sympathy toward strangers leads to a more substantive solidarity with neighbors because it turns some of those strangers into neighbors.[32]

From the Cruelty of the Dark Years to Solidarity Afterward

Part of what initiates the "dark years" involves the return of intense cruelty and institutional humiliation toward African Americans and Mexican Americans, the LBGTQ+ community,[33] and women. After the election of a "strongman," Rorty notes, there will be a severe regression in the way we talk and think about these groups of people.[34] Rorty gives us reason to believe that cruelty and humiliation toward these groups continues through the "dark years," and it seems reasonable to infer that the suburbanites who settle disputes with their neighbors through the use of guns are doing so in relation to racial dislikes and sexual distastes. If police officers can get away with shooting unarmed African-American men prior to 2020, then (within Rorty's set of predictions) perhaps white suburbanites will assume that they can get away with shooting African-American men from 2020–2045. As a result of the internationally aligned oligarchy, it seems probable that harshness will increase toward members of the LBGTQ+ community: Vladimir Putin's Russia already has strict laws against gays and lesbians, and he seems to be the leader of the international oligarchy.[35] What is the way out of this cruelty and humiliation?

The way out requires a process of re-enchantment through reading novels and Scripture. Because of novels and Scripture, American citizens simply stop living with fear and hate—which fuels the cruelty and humiliation—and broaden their sense of "us" and "we."[36] In Rorty's words: "Our

32. Ronald Kuipers also reads Rorty on these terms: "[O]ur only hope for an authentic and lasting solidarity rests upon our ability to reveal who we are in our distinctness, without our distinctness being immediately disqualified as out of place in public discussion. We must first be allowed to be strangers so that we may eventually become neighbours" (Kuipers, SS, 4).

33. As it happens, the same week that I am writing this chapter the Supreme Court is actually considering a case in which it might become legal to fire an employee if they identify with the LGBTQ+ community.

34. Rorty writes: "[T]he gains made in the past forty years by black and brown Americans, and by homosexuals, will be wiped out," and "[j]ocular contempt for women will come back into fashion" (Rorty, AOC, 90).

35. See Dawisha, *Putin's Kleptocracy*, ch. 7.

36. In the words of Ronald Kuipers: "Rorty . . . seem[s] to be saying that, in the border

sense of solidarity is strongest when those with whom solidarity is expressed are thought of as 'one of us', where 'us' means something smaller and more local than the human race."[37] The sympathy we have toward strangers will lead to solidarity with neighbors: some strangers become recognized as neighbors while the strangers that remain strangers will receive a heightened sense of sympathy.[38]

Ronald Kuipers describes Rorty's account of solidarity in terms of care, difference, and inclusion. First, according to Kuipers, "Rorty's crucial insight . . . is that solidarity is a product of a caring culture."[39] Second, according to Kuipers, Rorty insists "that . . . solidarity is the result of our ability to 'minimize differences' [and] wants to minimize, not obliterate, particular differences—differences, moreover, around which oppressive power imbalances are located."[40] Third, according to Kuipers, "[O]ur ability to create a more expansive sense of solidarity than presently exists shows that Rorty is aware that inclusion of the marginalized will also change how we think about ourselves and the culture from which we emerge."[41]

Eight years after the publication of *Contingency, Irony, and Solidarity,* in a 1997 essay, Rorty seemingly equates his use of solidarity with "justice." Steven Miller interprets Rorty's essay, "Justice as a Larger Loyalty," as Rorty attempting to update arguments from *Contingency, Irony, and Solidarity.* If solidarity happens when citizens start to talk and think more broadly about who to include in their own "us" and "we," then justice occurs when we treat the "them"s and the "they"s with fairness but without collapsing the differences between "us" and "them."

According to Miller, Rorty's emphasis on "us" and "we" comes from the American philosopher Wilfrid Sellars (1912–1989). In his book entitled *Science and Metaphysics,* Sellars makes the following argument:

---

country between my culture and the stranger's, I somehow discover that the stranger is not so strange after all—not so strange, at any rate, that I should exclude her from the blessings a liberal society has to offer. Once I am made to recognize that the other's difference should not make this kind of difference, I, with the rest of my culture, may easily sew those who are strange and unfamiliar onto the fabric of my familiar cultural vocabulary" (Kuipers, SS, 73).

37. Rorty, *CIS,* 191

38. In Rorty's words: "we try to extend our sense of 'we' to people whom we have previously thought of as 'they'" (Rorty, *CIS,* 192).

39. Kuipers, SS, 73.

40. Kuipers, SS, 73.

41. Kuipers, SS, 80.

> It is a conceptual fact that people constitute a community, a *we*, by virtue of thinking of each other as *one of us*, and by willing the common good *not* under the species of benevolence—but by willing it as one of us.[42]

Rorty comments, "[W]hat is essential is Sellars's idea that 'categorical validity' and 'moral obligation' can be identified with 'being willed as one of us', independent of questions about who *we* happen to be."[43]

Miller, however, claims that Rorty's adaptation of Sellars's "we" ought to be judged as only "quasi-Sellarsian." Why? Because "Rorty . . . seems more concerned about a community's moment of exclusion and boundary-setting rather than the inclusive framing that remained central for Sellars's understanding of community."[44] Because of his emphasis on "exclusion and boundary-setting," Miller argues that the "solidarity that Rorty has in mind . . . is local: to one's neighbors, to one's family, to one's trade union."[45] Miller continues, "He [Rorty] argues that an abstract conception of solidarity—i.e. to the human community—is a useless, inert fiction."[46] In conclusion, Rorty's notion of solidarity concerns a golden mean between a type of vicious tribalism and an unrealistic universalism.

FRATERNITY AND FRIENDSHIP IN LIFE AFTER THE DARK YEARS

Some strangers remain strangers; some strangers become neighbors; and some neighbors remain neighbors. In "Looking Backwards from 2096," however, Rorty writes the following about the latter half of the twenty-first century:

> Here in the late twenty-first century, as talk of fraternity and unselfishness has replaced talk of rights, American political discourse has come to be dominated by quotations from Scripture and literature, rather than from political theorists and social scientists. Fraternity, like friendship, was not a concept that . . . philosophers . . . knew how to handle. They could formulate principles of justice . . . , [b]ut how to formulate a 'principle of fraternity'? Fraternity is

42. Sellars, *Science and Metaphysics*, 222.

43. Rorty, *CIS*, 195.

44. Miller, *Community and Loyalty*, 76.

45. Miller, *Community and Loyalty*, 81.

46. Miller, *Community and Loyalty*, 81.

an inclination of the heart, one that produces a sense of shame at
having much when others have little.[47]

Do American citizens enjoy fraternity with both neighbors and strangers in
the latter half of the twenty-first century? What does fraternity have to do
with friendship (the only connection he makes between these two concepts
is to say that philosophers cannot "handle" them)? Does Rorty think that
fraternity will replace his earlier arguments for sympathy and solidarity?

My claim in the remainder of this chapter concerns how Rorty's
critique of philosophers—"Fraternity, like friendship, was not a concept
that . . . philosophers . . . knew how to handle"—applies to Rorty's own
predictions. On my interpretation of Rorty's predictions, fraternity is best
understood as his shorthand or singular word to capture his accounts of
solidarity and sympathy. His use of fraternity echoes the re-enchantment
I have developed: "Fraternity is an inclination of the heart."[48] In this sense,
fraternity does not replace solidarity and sympathy but becomes synonymous with what Rorty means by solidarity and sympathy. The concepts
of fraternity and friendship are neither synonymous nor interchangeable
within Rorty's political philosophy. Fraternity becomes shorthand for his
versions of solidarity and sympathy, and friendship turns out to be "a concept that" Rorty cannot "handle."

The critique of Rorty, which I develop in the remainder of this chapter,
is that friendship cannot and does not fit into Rorty's political philosophy.
The secular process of re-enchantment does not result in deep, healthy, serious friendships. Rorty's secular process of re-enchantment gets us only
from cruelty to solidarity and from shame to sympathy, which repeats the
limitations of neoliberalism when it comes to how we think of relationships
and what we expect from those closest to us.

The Work of Friendship

In my critique of Rorty's neglect of friendship, I return to Diane Rothleder's
The Work of Friendship—which I borrowed from earlier in this chapter to
outline the *work* of literature and novels within Rorty's thinking. Rothleder focuses on how Rorty's use of solidarity cannot and does not translate
into what she calls friendship as a kind of "particularized solidarity." In

47. Rorty, *PSH*, 248.
48. Rorty, *PSH*, 248.

her words: "Rorty makes particularized solidarity (i.e., friendship) problematic"—which means that Rorty's account of solidarity "needs some adjustment."[49] This adjustment concerns the pragmatist question "What is the *work* of friendship or what *work* might friendships do?" Rothleder claims, "The goal of the *work* of friendship is a friendship of *play*."[50] This "friendship of play" becomes her version of both a positive account of solidarity and a golden mean position between two problematic positions.

According to Rothleder, Rorty's notion of solidarity offers us only a *negative* version of solidarity. She argues, "Rather than constituting solidarity negatively . . . , Rorty needs a positive account of solidarity. Friendship is clearly one such account. Others are not seen as sufferers, but as joyous additions to life."[51] What does she mean by applying this negative/positive distinction to Rory's account of solidarity? She answers: "[W]e need a positive basis for solidarity—laughter and friendship, rather than Rorty's negative basis—collective fear of humiliation."[52] She adds the category of "play" to this answer as well: "To generalize friendship is to generalize laughter and play, clearly a more positive basis for solidarity than . . . the fear of humiliation."[53] Friendship, laughter, and play lead us to a *positive* account of solidarity.

She also argues that friendship of play allows us to "reach Rorty's goal of increased solidarity and decreased cruelty but without the isolation, alienation, and shame that seem to be at the heart of Rorty's [vision]."[54] She admits, however, that the phrase—"friendship of play"—captures an aspect of Rorty's thinking: "'[F]riendship of play' . . . signifies . . . a kind of practice that answers many of the [problems] leveled at Rorty, and at the same time, preserves much of what is right in Rorty's works."[55] How does "friendship of play" relate to what Rorty gets "right"? Her answer concerns Rorty's account of "redescription": "Within the context of friendship, accepting redescriptions from others is not only not humiliating, it can even be liberating or at least enjoyable."[56] Friendship of play gives us a way to

---

49. Rothleder, *WF*, 142, 143.

50. Rothleder, *WF*, 123.

51. Rothleder, *WF*, 143.

52. Rothleder, *WF*, xvii.

53. Rothleder, *WF*, 143.

54. Rothleder, *WF*, 42.

55. Rothleder, *WF*, 105.

56. Rothleder, *WF*, 141.

perform or practice Rorty's account of redescription, but it (friendship of play) also provides us with a positive version of solidarity that counters Rorty's negative version of solidarity.

Additionally, "friendship of play" allows us to come to terms with how friendship serves as a golden mean between communitarianism and individualism. Rothleder claims, "[T]he notion of friendship of play manages to avoid both . . . hyperindividualism . . . and the overly public hypercommunitarian[ism]."[57] She uses the word "hyperindividualism" to designate liberalism, whereas "hypercommunitarian" describes those reactions to liberalism that seek to recover ancient and/or medieval philosophy. Because of his private/public distinction, Rorty ends up defending both "hyperindividualism" and "hypercommunitarian[ism]." Instead, Rothleder argues, he should have looked for some golden mean between the two.

For Rothleder, this golden mean can be found in "friendship[s] of play" because "what friendships of play do is to make space for stories to be told, for people to feel connected"—which provides a response to the "need to have space in which to tell stories and play out roles."[58] Turning from Rorty's political philosophy to an account of friendship, however, might not be as easy as Rothleder suggests. Rorty's understanding of solidarity reflects tenets of neoliberalism, and neoliberalism puts restrictions on friendship.

The Problem of Neoliberalism

Neoliberalism reduces relationships to the figures of consumer or entrepreneur.[59] Todd May argues that this reduction applies not only to generic relationships within neoliberalism, but also to the particular relationship known as friendship.[60] In his *Friendship in an Age of Economics: Resisting the*

---

57. Rothleder, *WF*, 125.

58. Rothleder, *WF*, 127.

59. Or, in other words, "To live in a neoliberal world is to be encouraged to think of one's fellows in terms of [either] pleasure [or] profit" (May, *Friendship in an Age of Economics*, 118).

60. May writes: "For the consumer, friendships are relationships of pleasure, bringing entertainment or diversion to one's existence. For the entrepreneur, relationships are investments; they consist of interactions with others for the sake of some future goal in which those interactions are determined by the most efficient means of reaching that goal . . . . [W]hat neo-liberalism has accomplished is to give a particular economic inflection to the two types of lesser friendships that Aristotle describes, and then to encourage us to embrace them" (May, *Friendship in an Age of Economics*, 63).

Forces of Neoliberalism (2014), May mounts a book-length critique of how neoliberalism—the strange mix of capitalism and democracy that we have lived with (at least) since the early 1980s—negatively impacts friendships and our everyday relationships.[61] I borrow from his detailed and stringent critique but only those aspects of his critique that clarify and connect with Rorty's uses of solidarity and sympathy.

Using the categories of past, present, and future, May further develops what it means for neoliberalism to turn our relationships into the figures of consumer or entrepreneur. He writes,

> [T]he figure of the consumer is oriented toward the present. That is where the pleasure is. The figure of the entrepreneur, by contrast, is oriented toward the future, which is where the profit is. For neither figure does the past play a significant role. There is no pleasure or entertainment in the past, and nothing to be gained from a past that is no longer. Deep friendships, by contrast, require a past. The past does not have to be temporally extended: deep friendships can develop through a short but intense past. For there to be deep friendships, however, the past must play a founding role. The role it plays is not a nostalgic one; in fact, nostalgia often replaces communication in friendships that once might have been deep. Rather, its role is that of foundation for the friendship itself.[62]

According to May, deep friendships require a non-nostalgic account of the past. Nostalgia "replaces communication in friendships"—which seems to mean that nostalgia does not build from the past but, rather, wants to repeat or return to a past that is no longer there. Better put, the past is only there because it provides a shared experience and feelings that bind friendships together.[63] Because of the role of the past within deep friendships, neoliberalism pushes back against the development of deep friendships within American society.[64]

---

61. By "neoliberalism," May means "a set of themes and motifs that are privileged in our world, not a person who dominates it" (May, *Friendship in an Age of Economics*, 118).

62. May, *Friendship in an Age of Economics*, 93.

63. "There arise in friendships human feelings that bind people together, [but] neoliberalism . . . pushes against those human feelings . . . and may succeed in stunting them" (May, *Friendship in an Age of Economics*, 74).

64. "This is the pushback from neoliberalism against deep friendship: not its resistance to such friendship but the effects of its pervasiveness in molding us into beings for whom friendship is motivated by other concerns" (May, *Friendship in an Age of Economics*, 118).

May's use of the categories past, present, and future for describing relationships applies quite well to Rorty's understanding of solidarity and sympathy. For Rorty, sympathy seems oriented toward the present. It might turn out that, by sympathy, Rorty simply means allowing others to be as much of a "consumer" as everyone else is. Solidarity, for Rorty, is future-oriented.[65] The more people who enjoy and are welcomed into solidarity, the more profits for all of us. In May's words, "Entrepreneurial friendships can be altruistic . . . , but neoliberalism presses them in the direction of self-interest."[66]

Digging deeper into the relationship between friendship, solidarity, and sympathy, May demonstrates the limitations of solidarity and sympathy. Do his critiques of solidarity and sympathy apply to Rorty's understanding of solidarity and sympathy? Yes, they do. First, sympathy: May argues that deep friendships go beyond feelings of sympathy. He claims, "[A] friendship that rests solely on sympathy and without the possibility of growth and development cannot rise to the level of a close or communicating friendship."[67] May treats sympathy as an ingredient for the beginning of friendships, but a deep friendship moves beyond feelings of sympathy.

At one point, May seems to define a deep friendship on the terms of sympathy plus trust. He argues, "Trust and sympathy are not only instrumental to the self-development of friends; they are . . . crucial aspect[s] of the friendship itself, contributing in their own right to the meaningfulness of the friendship." Within neoliberalism, however, sympathy can be achieved but not trust because "[n]eoliberal relationships are economic ones . . . centered on consumption and investment"[68]—which means that, in neoliberalism, "there is no room for trust."[69] He continues, "neoliberalism pictures people as isolated individuals who occasionally come in contact with each other or one another."[70] At this point, we can see how Rorty's account of sympathy repeats neoliberalism in the sense that he defends a

65. "Entrepreneurial friends . . . are friends of usefulness in Aristotle's sense without being familiar friends . . . . In fact, for entrepreneurial friends, displays of vulnerability or personal exposure would most likely be deterrents to the development of the friendship. What entrepreneurs seek are go-getters, not support systems" (May, *Friendship in an Age of Economics*, 86).

66. May, *Friendship in an Age of Economics*, 79.

67. May, *Friendship in an Age of Economics*, 93.

68. May, *Friendship in an Age of Economics*, 108.

69. May, *Friendship in an Age of Economics*, 113.

70. May, *Friendship in an Age of Economics*, 113.

version of sympathy that does not come with room for trust. Rorty defends a version of "hyperindividualism," and this "hyperindividualism" encourages isolation and discourages trust.

For instance, "good white people" might have sympathy for those immigrants stuck on the Mexican border, but do we really think that they would trust them in their homes and neighborhoods?[71] Unfortunately, the only honest answer to this question is "no." This represents the lasting effects of neoliberalism, and it also captures—in a question—Rorty's political philosophy in the following sense: Rorty might decry cruelty, but he never suggests that we ought to become friends with those who experience cruelty.

Second, May also exposes the limitations of the concept of solidarity within neoliberalism. Making a stronger case against solidarity than he did against sympathy, May writes:

> [T]he intimacy of a close friendship not only does not prepare one for . . . solidarity but actually stands as an obstacle to it . . . . [D]eep friendships, because of their particular character, seem to turn one away from political involvement or solidarity. This can be for at least two reasons: the limited number of deep friendships one can have and the irreplaceability associated with them.[72]

When Rorty worries about "particularized solidarity" or vicious tribalism, he also—even if inadvertently—expresses concern about deep friendships.[73] To the extent that Rorty reflects or repeats patterns of neoliberalism, he worries about "particularized solidarity" or vicious tribalism because deep friendships present a challenge to the relationships allowed by and within neoliberalism. Although we can speak *against* vicious tribalism and *for* deep friendships, Rorty seems to equate the two with his refusal to go from the category of neighbor to that of friend. I agree with Dianne Rothleder that, on Rorty's terms, friendship would be defined as a kind of "particularized solidarity." In the end, Rorty's political philosophy disallows and discourages "deep friendships," "friendships of play," and "particularized solidarity."

---

71. For a philosophical explanation of the phrase "good white people," see Sullivan's *Good White People: The Problem with Middle-Class White Anti-Racism*.

72. May, *Friendship in an Age of Economics*, 124.

73. I take this to be one of the main points of Rothleder's *The Work of Friendship*.

CONCLUSIONS

I can make my critique in one of two ways, and I do both to please readers with different tendencies. On the one hand, I can say that Rorty's accounts of solidarity and sympathy fail because they do not get us to substantial versions of fraternity and friendship. Rorty promises fraternity as one of the characteristics of what our social hope looks like for the years 2045–2095, but he offers us no vision for what that entails. The significance of this failure concerns how Rorty's social hope ends up being yet another boring, problematic, and unhelpful (unhelpful is what matters most within pragmatism) defense of neoliberalism. If Rorty simply means by the "dark years" a time between two epochs of neoliberalism—1980–2013 and 2045–2095—then I will be the first to say that Rorty's social hope leads to despair because a repeat of neoliberalism is not an object worthy of hope.

On the other hand, and closer to my own tendencies as a thinker and writer, I can say that Rorty's accounts of solidarity and sympathy are helpful because they get the conversation started on what solidarity and sympathy look like and whether they must be determined by neoliberalism. I supplement Rorty's vision for fraternity with May's and Rothleder's explanations of friendship, and I urge that the social hope we ought to have post-"dark years" concerns a hope in deep, healthy, and playful friendships in addition to a hope in solidarity and sympathy. This critique, therefore, adds friendship to Rorty's account of solidarity and sympathy rather than substitutes solidarity and sympathy for fraternity and friendship.

What I resist, mostly, is allowing neoliberalism to determine our relationships. There is no hope in a return to neoliberalism. For all of the problems with the character and presidency of Donald J. Trump, I think we might look back at his election as a welcomed "end to neo-liberalism"—and Rorty might be right that we must go through some "dark years," some birth pangs, in order to finally "achieve our country."[74]

---

74. For the phrase "end to neo-liberalism," see Cornel West's "Goodbye, American Neo-Liberalism"; for the phrase "achieving our country," see James Baldwin, *FNT*, 105.

Chapter 5

Should We Sever Hope from Faith?
The Turn to 1 Corinthians 13

IN HIS DEFENSE AND explanation of the concept of hope in Richard Rorty's neo-pragmatism, John C. Adams writes:

> The story of rhetoric's risk—of its successes and failures—is the story of rhetoric's play as humans use and misuse symbols to project possible futures, to attend to what is not yet actualized but may be ever present as hope in life's mutable and mutating flow . . . . One of rhetoric's key movements is toward the future—toward what is not-yet—toward what cannot be known by any means, but can only be wisely and plausibly calculated. In a sense, rhetoric's engagement of discourse to set a course into the future is always vested in someway in hope and fear, in trust and belief.[1]

Building from these insights on the relationship between hope, rhetoric, and the significance of the future, I explore in further detail the concept of hope within Rorty's neo-pragmatism. I am interested, in particular, in what Rorty thinks about the future of religion—which he claims involves "hope without faith."

Should we sever hope from faith? Richard Rorty's answer to this question is a resounding "yes." Rorty claims "hope without faith" as his way to contribute to the philosophy of religion. Because of the category

---

1. Adams, "Hope, Truth, and Rhetoric," 81.

of hope, the intention of this claim involves being oriented toward the future instead of the past.

In this chapter, I first (and briefly) delineate Rorty's arguments for "hope without knowledge"—because they provide a lens for his more interesting defense of "hope without faith." Second, I explore Rorty's defense of "hope without faith" in relation to his predictions concerning the future of religion on the terms of pertinent arguments found in the work of Sigmund Freud and Martin Heidegger. I argue that Rorty's hope for the future of religion ought to be understood as a replacement of Freud's hope for the end of religion, and I employ Heidegger's distinction between anticipation and expectation in order to better understand what Rorty means by the *future* of religion (as well as what Adams—in the above quotation—means by "One of rhetoric's key movements is toward the future . . . toward what cannot be known by any means, but can only be wisely and plausibly calculated"[2]). As a whole, the argument of the chapter is built around Rorty's turn to a particular passage in the Christian canon: 1 Corinthians 13.

THE FUTURE OF POLITICS: HOPE WITHOUT KNOWLEDGE

Rorty defends his version of "hope without knowledge" in three of his writings: *Philosophy and Social Hope* (1998), "Pragmatism as Romantic Polytheism" (2005), and *An Ethics for Today* (published around the time of his death in 2007). I treat them out of chronological order: *Philosophy and Social Hope, An Ethics for Today,* and "Pragmatism as Romantic Polytheism." I read *An Ethics for Today* against itself—not as an argument "for today," as in the early twenty-first century, but as an argument for the latter half of the twenty-first century (2045–2095).

Hope without Knowledge: Rorty's Version of American Exceptionalism

In 1998, Rorty articulated two reasons why we should replace knowledge with hope. The first reason involves Rorty's critique of ancient philosophy. To say

2. Adams, "Hope, Truth, and Rhetoric," 81.

> 'Hope in Place of Knowledge' is a way of suggesting that Plato and
> Aristotle were wrong in thinking that humankind's most distinc-
> tive and praiseworthy capacity is to know things as they really
> are—to penetrate behind appearance to reality. . . . I want to de-
> mote the quest for knowledge from the status of end-in-itself to
> that of one more means toward greater human happiness.
>
> My candidate for the most distinctive and praiseworthy hu-
> man capacity is our ability to trust and to cooperate with other
> people, and in particular to work together so as to improve the
> future.[3]

The last sentence of this quotation signals Rorty's "hope": not knowledge
as "humankind's most distinctive and praiseworthy capacity" but, rather,
"our ability to trust and to cooperate with other people" for the purpose of
improving our future. Second, replacing knowledge with hope concerns
what Rorty thinks is a peculiar aspect of America. According to Rorty,
American politics ought to "substitute *hope* for the sort of knowledge
which philosophers have usually tried to attain" because "America has always been a future-oriented country."[4] Because of this orientation toward
its own future, political philosophy about America ought to put "hope in
place of knowledge." Because we cannot know the future, but either anticipate or expect it, then we have no choice but to think in terms of a hope
without knowledge.

Hope without Knowledge: Rorty's Defense of Globalization

In *An Ethics for Today*, however, Rorty goes beyond talk about political
philosophy for America. He uses his notion of hope without knowledge to
envision a "planetwide cooperative commonwealth" in the future.

In *An Ethics for Today*, Rorty distinguishes between hope with knowledge and hope without knowledge on these terms: "the hope to transcend
finitude" vs. "the hope for a world in which human beings live far happier
lives than they live at the present time."[5] The former type of hope—hope
with knowledge and "the hope to transcend finitude"—leads to "a vision of
vertical ascent toward something greater than the merely human," whereas
hope without knowledge leads to "a vision of horizontal progress toward

---

3. Rorty, *PSH*, xiii.

4. Rorty, *PSH*, 24.

5. Rorty, *An Ethics for Today*, 14.

a planetwide cooperative commonwealth."[6] Hope without knowledge is not confined to the American context but includes a particular vision for globalization. Because of the horizontal-vertical distinction, this particular vision for globalization not only results from a hope without knowledge but gives us more of a sense of hope without faith as well.[7]

In terms of the phrase "for today," Rorty's argument does not line up with what he says elsewhere—namely in his predictions—about American society and globalization. The argument in *An Ethics for Today* suggests that we will not have thirty years of darkness. Either Rorty changed his mind about his own set of predictions, or the argument in *An Ethics for Today* should be titled "An Ethics for 2045–2095." On the interpretation of Rorty's political philosophy developed within the present book, this either/ or leads me to affirm the latter option.

Hope without Knowledge: Romantic Polytheism

Richard Rorty's "Pragmatism as Romantic Polytheism" remains a neglected essay within scholarship on Rorty's neo-pragmatism and for good reason: it can be a confusing text to read. Rorty defends a position he calls "romantic polytheism" throughout the essay—which borrows insights about religion from John Dewey, William James, J. S. Mill, and Friedrich Nietzsche.

However, in the third section of "Pragmatism as Romantic Polythe- ism," Rorty claims that romantic polytheism borrows an ethics of love from Christianity as envisioned by the apostle Paul. Further, Rorty thinks the European Enlightenment makes it possible to universalize Paul's Christian love ethic. In "Pragmatism as Romantic Polytheism," Rorty connects the apostle Paul's view of charity with insights about religion found in the work of Dewey, James, Mill, and Nietzsche.

In addition to these strange bedfellows, Rorty wants "the relatively tolerant polytheism of the Roman Empire."[8] Paul, himself, thought that his so-called love ethic was necessarily in conflict with the virtues and vices required within Roman polytheism. Rorty does not tell us how he/we can have it both ways, but I find it deeply problematic that Rorty thinks Paul's love ethic—which Rorty calls the "only law" in the globalized

6. Rorty, *An Ethics for Today*, 17.

7. Rorty's *An Ethics for Today* also serves as a response to Nussbaum's critique of Rorty favoring patriotism over cosmopolitanism.

8. Rorty, PRP, 33.

future—non-problematically meshes with the "tolerant polytheism of the Roman Empire." Rorty's use of 1 Corinthians 13 in "Pragmatism as Romantic Polytheism" requires further scrutiny in relation to his use of 1 Corinthians 13 in other essays.

HOPE WITHOUT FAITH: THE FUTURE OF RELIGION

Hope without faith involves what Rorty thinks of the future of religion, and in this section I shift the phrase to be the *future for religion*.

For Rorty, Christianity offers two ways to achieve this hope without faith. First, the Christian text of 1 Corinthians—particularly the thirteenth chapter—provides a framework for understanding the primacy of charity and love. In this case, however, Rorty's hope does not reference the hope mentioned in 1 Corinthians 13, but, rather, Rorty's hope concerns the charity and love described in 1 Corinthians 13 without the faith and hope that accompanies such charity and love.

The second way that Christianity achieves a hope without faith is found in Rorty's adoption and interpretation of his maternal grandfather's social gospel theology. On Rorty's interpretation, Walter Rauschenbusch constructs a theology that shifts the meaning of Christianity from that of doctrine and faith to *praxis* and love. Scholars of Rauschenbusch's social gospel theology would most likely quibble with such a hard distinction, but Rorty seems to offer his interpretation on the grounds of a grandson claiming familial authority. In this case, Rorty finds in his maternal grandfather a type of theological reasoning that gives us concrete hopes with neither Christian doctrines nor Christian faith.

From Hope without Religion to Hope without Faith

According to Sigmund Freud, there is no future for religion. My explanation of Freud's argument in *The Future of Illusion* begins with the word "future" and then takes up "illusion." The argument that Freud presents in *The Future of Illusion* concerns the usefulness of religion in relation to the past, present, and future.

First, according to Freud, religion relies on a refusal to question the past. Freud writes, "If all the evidence put forward for the authenticity of religious teachings originates in the past, it is natural to look . . . and see whether the present . . . , which . . . is easier to form judgments [about], may not also be able to furnish evidence."[9] The past allows, continues, and determines "the future of an illusion"—that is, the "illusion" has a future as long as religious believers refuse to question the "past" that they inherit through their religious traditions. Second, the present moment—which Freud seems to think of as the twentieth century—ought to be a time of questioning religion because "it is easier to form judgments" about the present. We need to leave the past in the past, and we need to start questioning the beliefs that we inherit from the past—especially religious beliefs. Third, in the future, religion will be considered an "illusion"—which means that, on the terms of hope, Freud's hope for religion is that it will no longer be with us. In short, the past is no longer useful to us; the present becomes useful to the future *if and only if* we use the present to question the beliefs that we have inherited from the past.

If that is what Freud means by "future," then what does he mean by "illusion"? In *The Future of an Illusion*, he dedicates two pages to distinguishing between "illusion" and "delusion"; this distinction serves as our guide for understanding his use of "illusion." He concludes that religion is not a "delusion" but, rather, an "illusion." What are the differences?

Illusions:	Delusions:
Wish-Fulfillments	Contradict Reality
Neither Proven nor Disproven	Can Be Disproven
Neither True nor False	Never True, Always False

For Freud, religion will come to an end because we no longer need it as a "wish-fulfillment." Freud does not argue that religion will be proven false, either in the present or the future. Instead, religion will come to an end because what it has provided throughout time will no longer be needed by humanity. In the words of Elizabeth Rottenberg, "Freud ends up pointing [us] to something in reason itself that takes us beyond [both religion and science]."[10] There is no future for religion because "[w]hat lies in the future, says Freud, is the primacy of the intellect."[11] In this sense, Freud's hope that religion will no longer be with us should not be reduced to simply a negative hope about religion. Freud's hope is based more upon a positive hope

---

9. Freud, *Future of an Illusion*, 34.

10. Rottenberg, *Inheriting the Future*, 2.

11. Rottenberg, *Inheriting the Future*, 2–3.

in the maturity of humanity. Freud's hope "is the primacy of the intellect"[12] (more on this in chapter 6).

Not so for Rorty: what lies in the future is not the primacy of the intellect but the primacy of love. We learn this in Rorty's essay "Anticlericalism and Atheism," published in *The Future of Religion*. This love, better understood as Pauline charity, represents the "future of religion." By Pauline charity, I mean that Rorty envisions a future where both religious believers and nonreligious citizens will embody and practice what Paul wrote about charity and love in his letter to the church in Corinth in the first century:

> If I speak in the tongues of men and of angels, but have not love, I am a noisy gong or a clanging cymbal. And if I have prophetic powers, and understand all mysteries and all knowledge, and if I have all faith, so as to remove mountains, but have not love, I am nothing. If I give away all I have, and if I deliver up my body to be burned, but have not love, I gain nothing. Love is patient and kind; love does not envy or boast; it is not arrogant or rude. It does not insist on its own way; it is not irritable or resentful; it does not rejoice at wrongdoing, but rejoices with the truth. Love bears all things, believes all things, hopes all things, endures all things. Love never ends. As for prophecies, they will pass away; as for tongues, they will cease; as for knowledge, it will pass away. For we know in part and we prophesy in part, but when the perfect comes, the partial will pass away. When I was a child, I spoke like a child, I thought like a child, I reasoned like a child. When I became a man, I gave up childish ways. For now we see in a mirror dimly, but then face to face. Now I know in part; then I shall know fully, even as I have been fully known. So now faith, hope, and love abide, these three; but the greatest of these is love.[13]

Before I connect this to "hope without faith," we should make an observation that Rorty seemingly misses. Interestingly, Paul argues not for "hope without knowledge," but for love without knowledge: because of love, "knowledge . . . will pass away."

According to Rorty, this version of love will be the "only law" found "in a [future] global civilization." What will this "global civilization" look like when love becomes the "only law"? Rorty answers with this picture: "[C]ommunication [will] be domination-free, class and caste [will] be unknown, hierarchy [will] be a matter of temporary pragmatic convenience,

---

12. Rottenberg, *Inheriting the Future*, 2–3.

13. 1 Cor 13 (ESV).

and power [will] be entirely at the disposal of the free agreement of a literate and well-educated electorate."[14] When love is the "only law," then all communication will be free of deception and manipulation. When love is the "only law," then classes and hierarchies will cease. When love is the "only law," politics and power will be determined by the "literate and well-educated" without the need for dirty politics and scheming campaigns.

In the final paragraph of "Anticlericalism and Atheism," Rorty admits that he has "no idea how such a society could come about."[15] He calls it a mystery, but what kind of mystery can a former atheist defend? Rorty returns to 1 Corinthians 13 in order to answer this question:

> This mystery . . . concerns the coming into existence of a love that is kind, patient, and endures all things. 1 Corinthians 13 is an equally useful text for both religious people . . . whose sense of what transcends our present condition is bound up with a feeling of dependence, and for nonreligious people like myself, for whom this sense consists simply in hope for a better human future. The difference between these two sorts of people is that between unjustifiable gratitude and unjustifiable hope.[16]

According to Rorty, 1 Corinthians 13 provides common ground for religious believers and nonreligious citizens. The fact that he calls this a mystery means that a kind of re-enchantment will take place. This re-enchantment ought to be thought of as a secular version of re-enchantment that has as its end or *telos* charity, love, and sympathy.

Rorty recognizes that there are two different interpretations of 1 Corinthians 13 at play, but these differing interpretations do not prevent this Pauline passage from providing common ground. The two different interpretations are: (a) religious believers start with our present condition and move toward dependence on God or the church, whereas (b) nonreligious citizens start with our present condition and "simply . . . hope for a better future." The reason 1 Corinthians 13 provides common ground is that both interpretations share a vision for the world, and this vision is based upon Paul's description of love—a love "that is kind, patient, and endures all

---

14. Rorty, "Anticlericalism and Atheism," 40.
15. Rorty, "Anticlericalism and Atheism," 40.
16. Rorty, "Anticlericalism and Atheism," 40.

things."[17] This kind of love is what becomes the "only law" in Rorty's vision for his "descendants . . . in a global civilization."[18]

In a wonderful essay on the tensions between cosmopolitanism and patriotism, the American philosopher of law and political philosopher Martha Nussbaum calls out Rorty for his defense of national pride and patriotism.[19] Because of his defense of national pride and patriotism, she goes as far as to say that nowhere in his writings does he consider "the possibility of a more international basis for political emotion and concern."[20] In other words, Rorty's philosophy does not resolve the tensions between cosmopolitanism and patriotism but strengthens the side of patriotism over cosmopolitanism. For Nussbaum, this represents a problem.

On the contrary, I argue that Rorty's turn to 1 Corinthians can be interpreted as a shift from patriotism and the virtue of pride (found in *Achieving Our Country* and *Philosophy and Social Hope*) to cosmopolitanism and the virtue of love. Rorty's turn to 1 Corinthians provides a place within his writings where he does demonstrate concern for international politics. In his turn to 1 Corinthians, Rorty writes that his "sense of the holy . . . is bound up with the *hope* that someday" his "remote descendants will live in a global civilization in which *love* is . . . the only law."[21] Rorty's ultimate hope is not for and with the United States of America and its citizens showing national pride and patriotism toward America. Rather, his *ultimate* hope concerns a globalized future where neither patriotism nor pride bring citizens together but the law of love brings citizens of the world together.

With this argument, it seems that Rorty's turn to 1 Corinthians not only relates to his shift from atheism to anticlericalism but also relates to a shift from American "jingoism" to a global cosmopolitanism built on the Pauline notion of love—which serves as the "only law."[22] When Nussbaum

17. Rorty, "Anticlericalism and Atheism," 40.

18. Rorty, "Anticlericalism and Atheism," 40. Elijah Dann summarizes it in these terms: "Differences with Vattimo come down to his ability to regard a past event as holy, and [Rorty's] sense [is] that holiness resides only in an ideal future . . . . [Rorty's] sense of the holy . . . is bound up with the hope that someday, any millennium now, my remote descendants will live in a global civilization in which love is . . . the only law" (Dann, *After Rorty*, 190–91).

19. See Nussbaum, PC, 155–62.

20. Nussbaum, PC, 156.

21. Rorty, "Anticlericalism and Atheism," 40; emphasis added.

22. "Jingoism" is Nussbaum's word; see Nussbaum, PC, 161.

says that she sees in Rorty's work no "proposal for coping with this very obvious danger [of American jingoism]," I say that I see his move from pride and patriotism to love as the virtue that unites us globally as his ultimate hope—which he grounds in his interpretation and use of 1 Corinthians 13.

Anticipation vs. Expectation in Martin Heidegger's Philosophy

The problem with the argument in the previous section is that it suggests that this charity and love will define the future of religion in an expected way or with a type of inevitability. That is not the case. How can we speak of the future of religion if we cannot simply expect it to come about the way that Rorty envisions?

According to the German philosopher Martin Heidegger, there are two ways that we orient ourselves in relation to the future: anticipation and expectation.[23] For Heidegger, expectation remains passive—displaying neither control nor freedom over one's *future*. For Heidegger, anticipation becomes active—displaying both control and freedom over one's *future*. *If religion is to have a future, if there is a future for religion*—and here I alter the phrase from the future of religion to a future for religion—*then religious believers need to anticipate such a future.*

The future is not waiting for us to arrive in it. Rather, the future must be created; the future is what we make it. Religious believers and their traditions have some hard choices to make in the twenty-first century: *either* (a) continue using rhetoric of hate, such as supporting politicians and their policies that thrive on a fear of and hatred toward people of different color and races, (b) justify oppression and suffering for the sake of staying close to far Right political leaders and parties, and (c) keep theological ideas alive without testing and updating those ideas, such as the ban on women's ordination within the Roman Catholic church and more conservative Protestant denominations; *or* (a) utilize a rhetoric of love and practice acts of charity toward all people, (b) follow the Hebrew prophets and challenge oppression and suffering in all of its forms at the risk of losing political power, and (c) challenge traditional theological formulas and ideas for the purpose of changing certain doctrines or providing new reasons for old doctrines. If religious traditions continue with the first three choices, then religion will have no future—religious traditions will die, and religious believers will be the ones who have killed their own traditions.

23. See Heidegger, *Being and Time*, 227–57.

In the twenty-first century, neither modern science nor secularism can be blamed for the decline of religion in the Western world. In the twenty-first century, only religious believers ought to be faulted for the decline of religion. By continuing with the first three choices (listed in the previous paragraph), religious believers follow the script written by Friedrich Nietzsche in the nineteenth century: "God is dead, and we [the religious believers] have killed him!"[24]

The future must be made, and it can be made in a way so that religion has a future—a *future for religion*. It will be the latter three options that will keep religion alive: (a) utilizing a rhetoric of love and organizing practices of charity toward all people,[25] (b) following the language and logic of the Hebrew prophets and challenging oppression and suffering in all of its forms at the risk of losing political power,[26] and (c) challenging traditional theological formulas and ideas for the purpose of changing certain doctrines or providing new reasons for old doctrines.[27] If religious believers and whole traditions can *remake* themselves to present their beliefs and convictions on these terms, then religious believers and their traditions can *make* a future for religion.

Returning now to Rorty's view, the way to do this for Christians and the church involves thoroughly adopting his maternal grandfather Walter Rauschenbusch's so-called social gospel theology.[28] In "Looking Backward from 2096," Rorty writes: "In the churches, the 'social gospel' theology of the early twentieth century has been rediscovered."[29] This rediscovery forges a future for religion, particularly Christianity, because it empowers and guides Christians and churches for living out charity, justice, and love.[30] Rauschenbusch's social gospel theology, on Rorty's terms, leads us to charity and love without faith. Rauschenbusch's social gospel theology, according to Rorty,

24. Nietzsche, *The Gay Science*, §125.

25. This relates to Rorty's vision for religion.

26. This relates to Cornel West's prophetic pragmatism; see Goodson and Stone, *Introducing Prophetic Pragmatism*, ch. 2 and 8.

27. This relates to Peter Ochs's rabbinic or scriptural pragmatism; see Goodson and Stone, *Introducing Prophetic Pragmatism*, ch. 2 and 8.

28. Rorty's understanding of "social gospel" theology seems so reductive that he makes it (his grandfather's theological work) uninteresting. I return to this point in chapter 7.

29. Rorty, *PSH*, 249.

30. Interestingly, Rorty does not make predictions about Buddhism, Hinduism, Judaism, Islam, or any other religious tradition.

represents the only future for religion. Rorty wants a Baptist and Evangelical social gospel theology without the current beliefs and behavior of those who currently are Trump-supporting Baptists and Evangelicals.[31]

CONCLUSION: MAKING SENSE OF RORTY'S INTERPRETATION OF 1 CORINTHIANS 13

The Pauline logic in 1 Corinthians 13 is that love is the greatest of the three of faith, hope, and love. Rorty does not repeat this logic. Rather, Rorty's claim is that his hope is love—the kind of love that Paul defends—without the faith and hope also defended by Paul. In other words, Rorty's hope is Pauline love with neither Pauline faith nor Pauline hope. Rorty's hope is Pauline love severed from the faith and hope of Paul's own theology.[32]

How can Rorty have Pauline love severed from Pauline faith? A seemingly throw-away comment found in Rorty's early essay "Postmodernist Bourgeois Liberalism" offers a way to make sense of how Rorty can adopt Pauline charity without being required to adopt the rest of Paul's theology. Toward the end of the essay, Rorty defends the practice of picking-and-choosing from the Jewish and Christian traditions without being required to make a full commitment to the doctrines and logic of both of these traditions: "This Jewish and Christian element in our [secular] tradition is gratefully invoked by free-loading atheists like myself."[33] If Rorty re-wrote this sentence in the 2000s, he would change his language to "free-loading anti-clerics."

I think we should champion free-loading atheists, free-loading anti-clerics, and secularists to borrow and gain wisdom from the Jewish and Christian Scriptures without thinking that Jewish and Christian believers and scholars will claim that they are then committed to the full doctrines and logic of the Jewish and Christian traditions. As part of this wish, I

---

31. I continue with this thread in chapter 7.

32. Rorty remains a complex thinker. Right before he died, Rorty drops this bomb against St. Paul in a response to Jeffrey Stout: "In my 'perfect secular utopia' neither hopes of such rewards nor fear of such punishments would play any role in moral or political deliberation. There would still be theists of the sort . . . I . . . admire, but none of the kind [I] fear. There would be room for the sort of God worshipped by [William] James, [Alfred North] Whitehead, [Paul] Tillich, and [Cornel] West . . . , but none for the sort worshipped by St. Paul" (Rorty, "Response to Jeff Stout," 547).

33. Rorty, PBL, 202.

applaud Rorty's adoption and interpretation of 1 Corinthians 13.[34] In terms of 1 Corinthians 13, I would go further to say that the Rortyean free-loading atheists/free-loading anti-clerics have a hermeneutical leg up on those Christians who claim to read Paul's Epistles literally. In other words, I wonder when American Evangelical Christians—who claim to read Paul's Epistles literally—will catch on to the language and logic of 1 Corinthians 13 and catch up to Rorty's Christian love ethic. Perhaps it will be twenty-five or thirty years from now . . .[35]

34. "Yes" is my answer to Ronald Kuipers's question: "Can a 'freeloading atheist' . . . invoke such a particularly Judeo-Christian notion of justice, without assuming all the transcendental baggage that goes along with it?" (Kuipers, SS, 84).

35. Readers can skip to chapter 7 to read the argument that follows from this question.

PART 3

The Problem of Predictions

IN THIS THIRD PART of the book, I take a step back from the content and substance of Rorty's predictions and his thinking in order to consider the nature and problem of predictions (chapter 6) and to demonstrate—building from the conclusion of chapter 5—that American Evangelical Christianity ought to be given their share of the blame if we are indeed in the "dark years" (chapter 7).

Chapter 6

The Nature of Predictions

Is RORTY RIGHT OR wrong in his prediction of the "dark years"? In order to answer this question in the best and most honest way possible, I must attend to the nature and purpose of predictions in general. I bring Rorty's set of predictions back into the discussion when appropriate.

THE NATURE AND PURPOSE OF PREDICTIONS

There seem to be three strategies for or types of making predictions, but most authors identify only two. The two types usually identified concern the basic dichotomy between religion and science: namely religious prophecy and scientific forecasting. The third type that I add can be understood as somewhere in between these two types, and the question that drives this section is whether Rorty's predictions fall into this third type. If so, what does that teach us about the nature and purpose of Rorty's predictions?

Admittedly, I remain uncertain what to call this third type but will take some guesses throughout this chapter. The third type shares particular characteristics of both the religious and scientific types of prediction. Importantly, the third type also comes with significant differences from both. We can gain clarity on the three types by framing their characteristics first in the metaphysical terms of past, present, and future and second through the epistemological categories of certainty, knowledge, and reason.

Religious prophecy offers a complex relationship between the past, present, and future. The characteristics of the religious type of making predictions are as follows: (a) negative judgment on the present, (b) use of past sources of the law or wisdom in order to (c) make predictions about either a better, hopeful future or a despairing, horrible future.[1] Predictions about a better, hopeful future are based upon God's promises. These promises are found in the source of law and wisdom, which the Jewish and Christian traditions identify as divine revelation or Scripture. Predictions about a despairing, horrible future are based upon the continued actions and behaviors of God's people—the same actions and behavior that deserve negative judgment from the prophet.[2]

In terms of the categories of certainty, knowledge, and reason, religious prophecy involves both divine and human reasonings. As human beings, prophets reason in the following way: prophets *critique* and *diagnose* the sins of the present generation, *infer* how the law and other parts of divine revelation apply to the present generation, and *predict* how divine revelation informs us about the future. Divine reasoning comes into play because God *authorizes* and *empowers* the reasoning of the prophet in the sense that the prophet's reasoning remains grounded in divine revelation. A prophet cannot predict what is contrary to the words of Scripture. Divine revelation forms the prophet and the prophet's reasoning, and the tradition—in

1. For my account of the despairing, horrible future found in the Christian tradition, see my chapter "Left Behind? The New Testament and the American Evangelical Christian Justification for War."

2. In his essay on Rorty and prophecy, Sam Brody construes the relationship between past, present, and future within religious prophecy a bit differently than I do here. He writes, "When prophetic politics tells negative stories about the nation's past and present, it does this without ever implying that its society is irredeemable. Such an implication, in fact, would run deeply contrary to its core mission—calling the people to turn, i.e. to re-fashion themselves as moral agents . . . . The future they call for is not 'like' the past in the sense of romantic nostalgia, but it does invoke the past in order to recall the people to their own past promises. This is not so different from what Rorty himself does when he invokes Lincoln, Whitman, and figures like Herbert Croly. It is true that God's forgiveness is a crucial part of the 'turning' process—prophecy necessarily imagines that at *some* point, God will get involved. However, the primary agency of *teshuva* is and must always be human. It is when this conviction slips away that prophecy ceases to emphasize freedom and turns into apocalyptic . . . . Finally, due to its covenantal framework, prophecy must necessarily place constraints on novel performances—but so does Rorty, who wants Americans to be inspired to continual self-creation *in the direction of justice*, rather than in just any direction whatsoever. Rorty, however, claims that he cannot offer any grounds for this preference, and that to search for such grounds is to repeat the Platonist mistake" (Brody, "The Grounds of Prophecy," book forthcoming).

particular, the people who participate in that specific tradition—either listens to or refuses the message of the prophet. While religious prophecy strongly connects the present with the past and the future, the kind of certainty achieved within prophecy rests with God alone. Prophets may sound as if they possess certainty in terms of their judgments on the present and their predictions about the future, but there seems to be a theological necessity for epistemic humility because the prophet's authority and power come from God and remain with God. The more the role of the divine gets lifted up within prophecy, the more epistemic humility required by the prophet.

Rorty's predictions about American politics contain both similarities to and differences from religious prophecy. First, Rorty's predictions stem from a critique and diagnosis of the present generation; Rorty deliberately directs and limits his critique to the academic Left. Second, the problems of the academic Left do not require a theological discernment for predicting the future but seem more like a historical inevitability for Rorty. Third, Rorty draws from past sources of wisdom to correct the academic Left— namely the sources he romanticizes as the "Reformist Left"—but *does not use these sources to make promises about the future in his predictions*; Rorty seems to desire a particular future but predicts a future different from the one he desires. However, Rorty predicts the future that he desires but only after America goes through the future that Rorty laments. Fourth, Rorty's predictions about these "dark years" strangely resemble the despairing, horrible predictions about the future found in certain parts of the Christian tradition. Like some prophecies within the Christian tradition require a lengthy time of trials and tribulations, Rorty predicts that we must go through the "dark years" prior to enjoying a time when love and sympathy become the norm within the US. The philosopher of hope sets up his readers for hopelessness—or, more accurately, a deferred hope. Fifth, do Rorty's predictions come with epistemic humility? Do they need to come with epistemic humility since there is no role for divine reason and revelation within his predictions?[3] What does epistemic humility look like within political predictions? This set of questions will be better answered after we work through the characteristics of scientific forecasting.

Based on the methods of modern natural sciences, scientific forecasting uses simplistic connections between past, present, and future. Scientific forecasting involves the following characteristics: (a) abstracting patterns

---

3. Scripture does play a role in his predictions about 2045–2095 but not in the same way as it does for religious prophets.

from the past, (b) making predictions about the future based upon the patterns abstracted from the past, and (c) using the present to test previous predictions made based upon the patterns of the past and then adjusting other predictions in accordance with the information gained within the present.[4] In short: *abstracting* patterns, *making* predictions, *testing* the predictions that can be tested.

From numerous options, I select two examples of scientific forecasting because these two examples aptly and clearly depict the categories of certainty, knowledge, and ways of reasoning within the natural sciences. The two examples are astronomical and meteorological. As we experience on a daily basis, meteorological predictions come with less certainty but still are mostly accurate, whereas astronomical forecasting seems to achieve high levels of certainty—consider the accuracy of predicting eclipses. Scientists never miss an eclipse, either lunar or solar, and every eclipse that scientists predict turns out to be right. Predicting eclipses is an ancient practice,[5] but with the methods and tools of modern science we have 100 percent certainty with each eclipse predicted.[6] Meteorological predictions, however, rarely achieve 100 percent certainty. There are two basic reasons for why it seems that predictions about the weather are often wrong. First, a temporal reason: within the natural sciences, it turns out—perhaps counterintuitively—that short-term predictions are more difficult to make than long-term predictions. Within the natural sciences, predicting an eclipse one hundred years from now contains much more certainty than predicting tomorrow's weather does. Second, a spatial reason: it might be fairer to say that predictions about the weather are not wrong but, rather, miss the mark on the map. Oftentimes, meteorologists predict the right weather but not in the right place. The reason for this is that weather patterns change in ways that are quicker than what human beings can discern. This is also why it remains important to distinguish between climate and weather: climate

---

4. I agree with Nicholas Rescher when he argues that "forecasting" serves as a better word than "predictions" for understanding the nature of predictions within the natural sciences: "It is advantageous to confine the term *forecast* to that specific sort of prediction which foretells the occurrence or nonoccurrence of a particular concrete eventuation at a particular definite time . . . . A *forecast* is thus a definite prediction concerned with specific and concrete events." He continues that unlike predictions in general, forecasts are "definitely verifiable/falsifiable at some particular juncture of the ultimate course of events" (Rescher, *Predicting the Future*, 42–43).

5. See Griggs, "Predicting Eclipses."

6. Karl Popper claims: "It is a fact that we can predict solar eclipses with a high degree of precision, and for a long time ahead" (Popper, "Prediction and Prophecy," 454).

names the macro-reality of the planet, whereas weather names the micro-realities of specific regions. Predicting the future of the climate is more like predicting eclipses than like making meteorological predictions.

Rorty's predictions about American politics contain both similarities to and differences from scientific forecasting. First, Rorty does not seem to abstract patterns from history;[7] indeed, he does not follow the cyclical pattern laid out by Plato that democracies turn into tyrannies. Second, his predictions come across closer to the meteorological than the astronomical in the sense that the phrase "something will crack" sounds as if there is a 70 percent chance of rain and not the-eclipse-will-happen-on-November-16. Third, his predictions seem to make him adjust his own *hopes* in terms of politics and society. This similarity with the natural sciences is the reason for my claim—made in the Introduction—that, after Rorty makes his predictions (in *Achieving Our Country* and *Philosophy and Social Hope*), Rorty's political and social philosophy ought to be interpreted as what he envisions for the latter half of the twenty-first century. In other words, the failures of the academic Left—of Rorty's own people—serve as the current reality (a.k.a. the present) that requires Rorty to adjust his political and social philosophy as his *hope* for what will become reality from 2045–2095.

Perhaps most importantly: Rorty claims neither the degree of certainty that we find in scientific forecasting nor that his predictions are authorized and empowered by the divine—which we find in religious prophecy.

Predictions in Natural Sciences vs. Predictions in Social Sciences

In my judgment, one of the problems of making predictions in the social sciences concerns how the popular forms of social-scientific prediction-making claim that they can achieve as much certainty as predictions made within the natural sciences.[8] I tend toward the skepticism of the great twentieth-century philosopher of science Karl Popper when he claims: "The fact that we predict eclipses [in the natural sciences] does not . . . provide a valid reason for expecting that we can predict revolutions [in the

7. I concur with Patrick Baert's judgment about Rorty's thinking: "He [Rorty] laments [the] strongly held conviction that the past somehow holds the key for a glorious future, that the laws will hold tomorrow and the day after tomorrow as they have always done so in the past" (Baert, "Richard Rorty's Pragmatism," 145).

8. The three primary authors who represent this flaw are Dan Gardner, Nate Silver, and Philip Tetlock. Silver has built a career on making social-scientific predictions about American politics and the sport of baseball.

social sciences]."[9] Unlike Popper, however, I am not prepared to dismiss altogether the possibility for social-scientific predictions.[10] In this section, I borrow from Popper's skepticism but only for the purpose of clarifying the distinction between making predictions in the natural sciences and making predictions in the social sciences.

Karl Popper questions the assumed logic of social-scientific predictions. Popper claims that the "fact that we can predict solar eclipses with a high degree of precision" does not serve as a premise for thinking that the "task of the social sciences is fundamentally the same as that of the natural sciences—to make predictions, and, more especially, historical predictions."[11] Popper defines historical predictions as "predictions about the social and political development of [humankind]."[12] In sum, the more that making predictions in the social sciences follows or looks like making predictions in the natural sciences, the less persuasive they become.

Rorty's predictions seem to qualify, in Popper's terminology, as *"predictions on a large scale."*[13] What does Popper mean by this? By *"predictions on a large scale,"* Popper means "long-term predictions whose vagueness is balanced by their scope and significance."[14] Vagueness becomes, for Popper, one of the main problems with social-scientific predictions—which means that making *"predictions on a large scale"* remains problematic on Popper's standards. The only positive claim made by Popper about social-scientific predictions involves a contrast between achieving in-depth meaning and vagueness: "Although social science in consequence suffers from vagueness, its qualitative terms at the same time provide it with certain richness and comprehensiveness of meaning."[15] Because of this "richness and comprehensiveness of meaning," Popper concludes this part of his analysis by saying: "[I]f long-term forecasts are at all attainable by the social sciences,

---

9. Popper, "Prediction and Prophecy," 457–58.

10. I concur with Nicholas Rescher's judgment about Popper's skepticism: "Overall, however, Popper pushes an otherwise sensible position too far." How so? "To reject a global historical dererminism . . . is all very well. But to say flatly that history cannot predict is plainly false" in the sense that "[m]any safe predictions can certainly be made in the human domain and many significant developments in human affairs can clearly be foretold with substantial accuracy" (Rescher, *Predicting the Future*, 206).

11. Popper, "Prediction and Prophecy," 454.

12. Popper, "Prediction and Prophecy," 455.

13. Popper, *Poverty of Historicism*, 33; emphasis in original.

14. Popper, *Poverty of Historicism*, 33.

15. Popper, *Poverty of Historicism*, 33.

then it is fairly clear that they can only be . . . large-scale forecasts"—as opposed to short-term predictions.[16] With this initial conclusion, it seems that Popper provides a justification for Rorty's social-scientific-based predictions. In the end, however, Popper thinks "large-scale forecasts"—within the social sciences—that turn out right are best understood as a type of political or social "miracle" that requires denying both human reason and *the power of bringing about a more reasonable world.*"[17]

We need not share Popper's final conclusion in order to learn from his analysis some clarifying distinctions between making predictions within the natural sciences vs. the social sciences. First, predictions in the natural sciences come with more certainty and clarity; predictions in the social sciences contain uncertainty and vagueness. Second, predictions in the natural sciences are more detail-oriented, whereas predictions in the social sciences seem to be directed toward developing in-depth meanings. Third, justifying making predictions in the social sciences should neither borrow from nor rely on the justifications and rationale for making predictions in the natural sciences. We might achieve this distinction by shifting from a truth-based expectation found in the natural sciences to an aesthetic-based judgment—which would result in the following distinction. Predictions made within the social sciences ought to be considered as the *art of making predictions*; the language of the *science of making predictions* ought to be avoided within the social sciences.

Do Rorty's predictions align with these features for social-scientific prediction making, for the art of making predictions? Yes to the first feature: Rorty's predictions contain many uncertainties and remain vague. The

16. Nicholas Rescher disagrees with Popper on this point. Instead, Rescher argues that short-term predictions are more likely. Either way, Rescher ultimately dismisses the possibility for making political predictions when he writes: "To think that we shall ever be in a position reliably to forecast next year's newspaper headlines is pie in the sky. Even routine short-term predictions in politics—election outcomes as a prime example—are hard to forecast with unqualified confidence. And the longer term is imponderable. *For elections eight or ten years down the road, we cannot say who the candidates will be, let alone which of them will win* . . . . [P]olitics is too volatile and chancy a process for confident prediction. It would be a foolhardy thing to place much reliance on the declarations of a seer who claimed to be able to forecast political developments in national or international affairs" (Rescher, *Predicting the Future*, 201; emphasis added). Rescher's book was published the same year as Rorty's *Achieving Our Country*, so it is unlikely that Rorty read Rescher's critique and dismissal of making political predictions. I must admit, however, that when I first read Rescher's paragraph I immediately thought: "Rorty read this paragraph and then said, 'Hold my beer.'"

17. Popper, *Poverty of Historicism*, 45; emphasis in original.

clarity of the predictions presented in this book ought to be considered as a Peircean exercise in trying to clarify a vague argument through intellectual distinction and rational reconstruction.[18] Rorty, himself, celebrates the fact that his writings fail to achieve certainty.

Yes to the second feature: Rorty's predictions are not detail-oriented but, rather, display his ability to paint with a broad brush in ways that develop in-depth meanings and a particular vision for "achieving our country" (James Baldwin's phrase, to be defended in the Conclusion). Yes to the third feature as well: Rorty neither borrows from nor utilizes any aspect of the truth-based expectations found within the natural sciences.

On the one hand, Rorty's predictions seem like the kind of political and social "miracle" discussed by Karl Popper (and Popper uses this language to dismiss the possibility of calling social-scientific predictions legitimate or real *predictions*). On the other hand, the predictions found in Rorty's *Achieving Our Country* and *Philosophy and Social Hope* make sense in terms of aesthetic reasoning: because of the failures (ugliness) of the academic Left, the broader population will turn toward a "strongman" (monster) to save them (as Trump offered and promised to do during the 2016 National Republican Convention). Rorty's predictions after the 2016 presidential election simply follow down an aesthetic path of how the US will grow uglier and uglier—as described in chapter 2. The phrase "dark years," itself, can be understood as an aesthetic claim because "darkness"—in Rorty's use of it—suggests a lack of proper perception. It involves, in particular, lacking the ability to appreciate and see.[19]

In conclusion, Rorty's predictions align with the stated features of social-scientific prediction-making. If we desire a name for Rorty's type of predictions, then they can be called historical predictions—"predictions about the social and political development of [humankind]."[20]

Predictions in Social Sciences vs. Predictions in Theology

If Rorty's predictions cannot be scientific, then why not give in to the usual dichotomy between religion and science and label Rorty's predictions as *prophetic*? This certainly is tempting, especially given that I have argued

18. See Peirce, "How to Make Our Ideas Clear," 124–40.

19. Traditionally, "seeing" serves as the perception that helps us make better and more refined aesthetic judgments about ourselves and the world.

20. Popper, "Prediction and Prophecy," 455.

elsewhere that Rorty's neo-pragmatism can be considered a weak version of *prophetic* pragmatism.[21]

Another reason to affirm this question concerns the label of historical predictions, which we concluded fit Rorty's set of predictions. In a different book (*The Poverty of Historicism*) than the one discussed previously, Popper furthers his discussion of historical predictions by developing a critique of historical prophecy. The definition of historical prophecy builds from the definition of historical predictions: "the prophecy of social, political, and institutional developments."[22] Popper says prophecy involves any "case we are told about an event which we can do nothing to prevent.... Its practical value lies in our being warned of the predicted event, so that we can sidestep it or meet it prepared."[23]

Elsewhere (*The Open Society and Its Enemies*), however, Popper argues that side-stepping a "predicted event" becomes nearly impossible because of the religious nature of prophecy. According to Popper, religious prophecies help bring about their own predictions. For Popper, this means that if such predictions turn out right it should not lead to the judgment that religious prophecy has some kind of "scientific character." Rather, in Popper's words, "[i]t may ... be a consequence of its religious character and a proof of the force of the religious faith which it has been able to inspire in [humanity]."[24] Historical prophecies look "scientific" because they are often right; however, they are not right in any "scientific" sense because their rightness cannot be separated from their "religious character." Their "religious character" leads history and humanity in such a way that it ensures the predictions come true. Similar to his dismissal of historical predictions as legitimate and real predictions, Popper concludes that historical prophecies—because of their "religious character"—fail the standards of legitimate and real predictions. The difference between his two judgments concerns how historical predictions are illegitimate despite borrowing from and relying on making predictions in the natural sciences, whereas historical prophecies ought to be deemed illegitimate despite the fact that they often come true—predictions coming true occurs with predictions made within the natural sciences.

---

21. See Goodson and Stone, *Introducing Prophetic Pragmatism*, ch. 8.

22. Popper, *Poverty of Historicism*, 40.

23. Popper, *Poverty of Historicism*, 38.

24. Popper, *Open Society and Its Enemies*, 401–2.

With the exception of the "Second Great Depression," Rorty's predictions about 2014–2020 have come true. Does this mean that Rorty's predictions take on a "religious character"? This question leads to a better and deeper understanding of Rorty's predictions because in no way do Rorty's predictions have the kind of "religious character" described by Popper. Rorty has neither the authority nor the community of followers that worked to ensure that his predictions come true. Rorty did not spend his energy, after 1999, doing whatever it took to bring us closer to his predictions. If we remain with Popper's terms, then Rorty's predictions can be categorized either as historical predictions or historical prophecies. If making predictions and working to bring about such predictions are required for prophecy, however, then Rorty's predictions do not qualify as historical prophecies.

Nevertheless, this conclusion does not mean that I am relinquishing the argument made in *Introducing Prophetic Pragmatism*—namely that Rorty's neo-pragmatism can be considered a weak version of prophetic pragmatism. In that book, I write:

> To call Rorty's version of prophetic pragmatism "weak" simply means that Rorty calls for cultural and political changes but with foundations neither for critiquing culture and politics nor a strong sense of where justice leads us into the future . . . . Rorty's neo-pragmatism can be considered a version of prophetic pragmatism because he rejects the status quo and hopes that love becomes "the only law."[25]

I can maintain that description of Rorty's prophetic pragmatism *and* claim now—without contradiction—that Rorty's predictions about the future are not prophetic because prophetic pragmatism is as much about critiquing the present as it is about predicting the future. Rorty critiques the present plenty, even if his criticisms are neither as deep nor as strong as others.[26]

Furthermore, Rorty's predictions about the years between 2045 and 2095 fit better with the predictive nature of prophetic pragmatism because those sets of predictions made by Rorty are *hopeful*. Rorty's predictions

---

25. Goodson and Stone, *Introducing Prophetic Pragmatism*, ch. 8.

26. In *Introducing Prophetic Pragmatism*, I differentiate Rorty's weak version of prophetic pragmatism from Cornel West's strong version of prophetic pragmatism and Peter Ochs's deep version of prophetic pragmatism.

concerning thirty years of darkness are not hopeful but despairing. More on this in the Conclusion.

Returning to my question—if Rorty's predictions cannot be "scientific," then why not give in to the usual religion-science dichotomy and label Rorty's predictions as *prophetic?*—my final answer builds from the discussion in the previous section. Because Rorty's predictions align with the stated features of social-scientific prediction-making, these features must be distinguished also from making predictions based upon theological reasoning. Rorty relies on neither divine promises nor divine revelation for making and thinking through his predictions. Although his predictions oddly sound like the trials and tribulations predicted by some American Evangelical Christians, his source for the "dark years" is not the final book of the New Testament—the book of Revelation—as it is for them.[27] Rorty's predictions may sound prophetic, especially his prediction concerning the election of a "strongman" in the 2016 presidential race, but calling them prophetic in the end miscategorizes Rorty's ways of reasoning found in his set of predictions.

Historical Predictions, Religious Prophecy, Scientific Forecasting

My preferred terms for the three strategies or types of predictions are scientific forecasting, religious prophecy, and historical predictions. I remain content with Karl Popper's label of historical predictions for what it means to make predictions within the social sciences—which is what Rorty does in *Achieving Our Country* and *Philosophy and Social Hope*. I differ from Popper on what to call the other two types of predictions, and I propose my own description of the three types of predictions.

27. Interestingly enough, the source of the trials and tribulations for American Evangelical Christians is not always the book of Revelation but the fictional series known as Left Behind (see Goodson, "Left Behind?")

Scientific Forecasting

Natural Sciences

Uses the present to test previous predictions

Views the past as the exhibition of patterns in the natural world

Degrees of certainty in relation to the type of prediction made
(our examples: predicting eclipses vs. predicting the weather)

Inferences made on the basis of the scientific method

Religious Prophecy

Theology

Offers negative judgments on the present

Views the past in terms of its sources of wisdom

Certainty remains with the divine; prophets must maintain epistemic humility

Inferences made on the basis of divine promises and divine revelation

Historical Predictions

Social sciences

Offers negative judgments on the present

Views the past as the exhibition of patterns in the social world

No degree of certainty; those who make predictions must maintain epistemic humility

Bases for inferences vary depending on methodologies within social-scientific
discipline

ENLIGHTENMENT PHILOSOPHY AND HISTORICAL PREDICTIONS

In his philosophical study concerning the nature of predictions, Nicholas Rescher outlines "the four major sorts of views" relating to the possible "structural trends and tendencies of history":

> *progressive*: matters are moving to a new and totally different—and better—order of things. . . .
>
> *retrogressive*: matters are in a state of decay moving back to a simpler, cruder, and more primitive order of things. . . .
>
> *stabilitarian*: fundamentally, things remain pretty much the same over the course of time. . . .
>
> *cyclic*: there is ongoing change; it does not have a fixed direction but moves in a repetitive pattern of ebbs and flows. . . .[28]

28. Rescher, *Predicting the Future*, 203.

We noted earlier that Rorty denies the cyclic view, and his predictions reveal to us that he does not hold to any type of stabilitarianism. Rorty boldly defends a notion of moral progress.[29] Because of his belief in moral progress, and because of his predictions concerning the "dark years," Rorty's predictions fit into the first two of the categories identified by Rescher: progressive and retrogressive.

His prediction concerning thirty years of darkness fits with the retrogressive view, and his prediction that solidarity and sympathy rule our political and social relationships from 2045–2095 fits with progressivism. Rorty explicitly defends the progressive view toward the end of *Contingency, Irony, and Solidarity*—published in 1989. Because of the retrogressivism of his predicted "dark years," overly simplistic claims—such as this one found in Ronald Kuipers's *Solidarity and the Stranger*, "Rorty thinks we can only look back at our past and compare the ways in which our present culture is more inclusive"—are not warranted.[30]

Rescher identifies philosophical schools of thought with each of the categories.[31] He mentions "Enlightenment thinkers" with the progressive view, and he names "Fin de siècle theorists" with the retrogressive view. What does it mean that Rorty mixes these two views, and what does it tell us about the nature and problems of Rorty's predictions?

I have three quick answers to the first question. First, the retrogressivism nuances—but does not cancel out—Rorty's progressivism. Although Rorty defends liberal and moral progressivism, the reterogressivism means that his progressivism cannot be interpreted on the standards of the caricature of liberal and moral progressivism. Second, Rorty makes his social hope (progressivism) dependent upon a time of despair—a stage when we move "back to a simpler, cruder, and more primitive order."[32] (This dependence is what I seek to continually challenge throughout the present book.) Third, Rorty's prediction found in the "something will crack" passage reveals that—at least, philosophically speaking—the slogan "Make America Great Again" ought to be judged as unapologetically retrogressive.

29. "[T]here is such a thing as moral progress, and that this progress is indeed in the direction of greater human solidarity . . . . [I]t is thought of as the ability to see more and more traditional differences (of tribe, religion, race, customs, and the like) as unimportant when compared with similarities with respect to pain and humiliation—the ability to think of people wildly different from ourselves as included in the range of 'us'" (Rorty, *CIS*, 192).

30. Kuipers, *SS*, 74.

31. See Rescher, *Predicting the Future*, 203.

32. Rescher, *Predicting the Future*, 203.

The second question, what does it tell us about the nature and problems of Rorty's predictions, cannot be answered so quickly. To initiate an answer to it, I begin from Rescher's identification of progressivism with Enlightenment philosophy and develop what such a connection means for the social-scientifically based type of predictions I have labeled as historical predictions. With the help of Elizabeth Rottenberg's *Inheriting the Future* (2005), Rorty's liberal and moral progressivism can be connected with the conception of the future found within the tradition of Enlightenment philosophy. Rorty tends to deny his indebtedness to this tradition,[33] but his liberal and moral progressivism places him squarely within this tradition.

Within the Enlightenment philosophical tradition, conceptions of the future are tied to the categories of humanity and inhumanity. In other words, Enlightenment thinkers use their conceptions of the future to judge the rationality of humanity. Rorty tells his readers over and over, however, that he does not fit into the tradition of Enlightenment philosophy precisely because of these types of judgments—the Enlightenment emphasis on rationality and reason. According to the philosophical story told by Elizabeth Rottenberg, however, Enlightenment thinkers do not always acknowledge how categories beyond reason come into play in their strong defenses of rationality and reason.

The primary thinkers within Rottenberg's philosophical story are Immanuel Kant and Sigmund Freud. She argues that Kant allows for both the faculty of the imagination and the faculty of reason to play a role within his conceptions of the future. In his essay "What Is Enlightenment?" he employs only the faculty of reason to judge humanity—both in the present and in the future.

Freud follows Kant's "What Is Enlightenment?" more strictly—which means that Freud *explicitly* allows only the faculty of reason to play a role within his conception of the future. Rottenberg writes:

> For Freud, our best hope is that the intellect—"or let us call it by the name that is familiar to us, reason"—may in time establish "a *dictatorship* in the mental life of man . . . ." The powers of reason must dispel . . . illusions . . . in order to lay the foundation of a new community—a community bound by reason."[34]

---

33. See Rorty, "Enlightenment and 'Postmodernism,'" 19–37.

34. Rottenberg, *Inheriting the Future*, 20. In chapter 5, we learn that the "illusions" referenced here concern "the illusions of religion."

For Freud, we should place our hope in human rationality and reason—to the point in which reason fully dictates "the mental life" of all humanity. Ultimately, our hope concerns "a new community—a community bound by reason" alone. This hope for a new community "bound by reason" depicts Freud's version of progressivism.

Rottenberg argues, however, that Freud downplays a crucial element that must be part of his conception of the future—an element that is beyond reason (hence my use of the word explicitly in the paragraph above). She calls it the "binding" or the "bond" that holds together this "new community": "a community *bound* by reason." This "binding" must be beyond reason because Freud thinks of human sociality in terms of destruction, impulsiveness, and violence. With a witty turn of phrase, Rottenberg claims that a "community bound by reason owes its binding force . . . to an energy . . . unbound."[35] Rottenberg's interpretation of Freud's role within the tradition of Enlightenment philosophy is exactly right, and my claim is that *Rorty fits into this tradition concerning a progressive conception of the future when it comes to light that there are aspects that go beyond relying-on-reason-alone within this tradition.*

She concludes that both thinkers (Kant and Freud) use their conception of the future to ground their judgments about humanity—humanity in the past, in the present, and in the future. What does she mean by this, and how does it relate to Rorty's predictions? She means that the future we inherit will teach us that we, in the present, are either *human* or *inhuman*. If we qualify as *human* now, on the terms of Enlightenment philosophy, then the future we inherit will be one of progress: a future deemed rational and reasonable on the standards of Enlightenment philosophy. If it turns out that we are *inhuman* now, then the future we inherit will be of our own making: "acts of cruelty, wanton violence, [and] those things we condemn—or monstrosize—as 'inhuman.'"[36] She continues,

> [T]hese inhuman elements simultaneously bequeath to us a future insofar as they promise us possibility beyond the possibilities of cognition. The inhuman is our future, I argue, not because we must learn to tolerate violence and atrocity but because the future would have no life without the risk of a certain inhumanity.[37]

35. Rottenberg, *Inheriting the Future*, 20.
36. Rottenberg, *Inheriting the Future*, 124.
37. Rottenberg, *Inheriting the Future*, 124.

This paragraph represents another way to describe what Rorty calls the "dark years" of American politics and society: a period of American history that will be characterized by atrocity, cruelty, and violence. While Rottenberg places the blame universally, on all of us, my claim is that Rorty places the blame more locally—specifically on the academic Left. In relation to Rottenberg's argument, Rorty wants to have it both ways: both the progressive future (2045–2095) and the inhuman future (2014–2044). Rorty uses the future to judge us now, and he also uses the future to tell us "everything will be okay."

What does it mean that Rorty boldly predicts the politics of the twenty-first century—from 2014 through 2095? In my judgment, such bold predictions place Rorty in a philosophical tradition that makes him uncomfortable—the tradition of Enlightenment philosophy. If I am wrong and it's not that tradition, then it seems that the other option (since Rorty clearly is not a scientific forecaster) is where Brad Elliott Stone places Rorty's thinking: in the tradition of the Hebrew prophets.[38] Either way, *Rorty's predictions about the twenty-first century leave him in the company he sought to avoid throughout the entirety of his career: either Enlightenment philosophers, who place too much faith in reason, or religious prophets, who put too much faith in faith.*

THE PROBLEM OF RORTY'S PREDICTIONS

The problem of these predictions is what it means to say that Rorty might be *right*. On the one hand, it seems remarkable that Rorty identified how the 2016 presidential election would go and the proliferation of gun violence— which we are currently experiencing. On the other hand, why would anyone—much less a philosopher and professor—predict events that become so lamentable and tragic?

Rorty predicts deep tragedies within American life. Why make predictions that we ought to wish will not come to fruition? Philosophically, this involves an epistemological dilemma: claiming to know future events that we cannot know and, furthermore, wishing that we did not know. Of course, Rorty spent a career debunking such philosophical approaches to knowledge. What is more pertinent, however, from Rorty's writing career involves his understanding of the future. For Rorty, the future is made by us; the future is not out there waiting for us to enter into it. There is no

---

38. See Stone, "Hope without Prophecy?"

future to know independent of the future that we make for ourselves. Why is this the future that Rorty knows, in the sense of predicting it, when there is no future yet to know?

Well, it must mean that Rorty's predictions are not claims of knowledge about what awaits us. Rather, Rorty's predictions concern what he thinks we are making ourselves. We bring about the "dark years"; we *make* the thirty years of darkness.

In this way, Rorty is not necessarily making predictions but performing diagnostic work on the future we make for ourselves as Americans. In other words, Rorty's seeming predictions demonstrate the peak of his pragmatism (as a branch of consequentialism, pragmatism emphasizes the consequences of beliefs and concepts): judging the present based upon the formulation of hypotheses about the consequences of the present. These consequences comprise what we consider the future, and perhaps the logic of pragmatism changes the way we ought to think about what we mean by the future. The future is not out there waiting for us to arrive in it. Instead, the future becomes the consequences—both intended and unintended—of the present. In this sense, Rorty spells out the consequences of the behavior and choices of the academic Left more so than making predictions about the future. However, we may continue to call them predictions so long as we understand them as taking guesses about the consequences of the present. Within pragmatism, we ought to redefine the practice of making predictions as a form of hypothesis-making about the consequences of actual and present events.

Nevertheless, Rorty's predictions remain problematic from a pragmatist perspective.[39] My final claim for this chapter is that *it does not matter if Rorty's predictions are right or wrong*. What matters is the pragmatist judgment about the *usefulness* of Rorty's predictions. What's the use of predicting thirty years of darkness and then fifty years of love and sympathy on a global scale?

---

39. I further develop this argument in the Conclusion.

Chapter 7

The Dark Years as Faith with Neither Hope Nor Love

To ANSWER THE QUESTION from the previous chapter: *Rorty's predictions become useful, not as predictions about the future, but as judgments against the present problems and tendencies concerning the academic Left.* Is this the only judgment we should make about present problems and tendencies? In this chapter, I explore an answer to who else might deserve judgment.

In order to accomplish such a task, I linger on questions concerning hope and love within the "dark years." I shift the blame for the "dark years" from the academic Left to American Evangelical Christianity and their support of Donald J. Trump as the object of their faith in American politics. More accurately, I think the blame should be shared between (a) the neglect of the working poor and the unemployed by the academic Left and (b) the temptation for political power found within American Evangelical Christianity—which makes it come across as more *American* than *Christian*

This chapter proceeds as follows. I begin with a critique of Rorty's hope in the work of his grandfather, Walter Rauschenbusch, and then (secondly) transition to a full diagnosis of American Evangelical Christianity. This diagnosis leads to the conclusion that the best way to understand American Evangelical Christianty in its present manifestation involves the judgment that American Evangelical Christians practice faith with neither

hope nor love—which is how this chapter connects with the previous section of the present book. Third, this chapter represents my own turn away
from Rorty's secular neoliberalism to Stanley Hauerwas's Christian postliberalism.[1] Such a turn involves connecting what I call pedagogical hope with
ways in which professors and scholars can and should begin thinking about
poverty in their classrooms and writings.

FROM RAUSCHENBUSCH'S SOCIAL GOSPEL
THEOLOGY TO HAUERWAS'S POSTLIBERALISM

Rorty favors the theology of his maternal grandfather, Walter Rauschenbusch,
but in doing so neglects contemporary sources of theological reasoning that
better relate to Rorty's own style of thinking and writing. Rauschenbusch's
social gospel theology has been both carried on and critiqued more by the
Gilbert T. Rowe Professor of Theological Ethics at Duke Divinity School and
Professor of Law at Duke University (now Emeritus in both positions), Stanley Hauerwas, than by any other living thinker and writer.

This claim will be controversial among both critics and defenders
of Hauerwas's theological reasoning, but evidence for this claim can be
found in Hauerwas's own words. He writes, "Walter Rauschenbusch was
an evangelist for the kingdom of God," and his thought is as "desperately
needed in our day as it was in his."[2] Hauerwas continues, "The passion for
justice, his prayers for social awakening, the hymns of social solidarity, and
the institutions for humane care he created cannot be taken for granted."[3]
Hauerwas concludes, "The work he began we must continue" because after
Rauschenbusch, "there is no gospel that is not 'the social gospel'. We are
permanently in his debt."[4]

Furthermore, in his book *A Better Hope: Resources for a Church Confronting Capitalism, Democracy, and Postmodernity*, Hauerwas dedicates
a whole chapter to Rauschenbusch's work. Hauerwas's understanding of

1. As it happens, the only occasion where I personally met and talked with Rorty,
Stanley Hauerwas was the one who offered the introduction. After being introduced,
the only statement Rorty made to me was: "My career advice to you is to never agree to
lecture or teach at a Mennonite college because they pay you shit." This advice came both
from left field and unsolicited, and the only inference I can make about it is that Rorty
was passive-aggressively critiquing Hauerwas's relationship with Mennonites.

2. Hauerwas, "Repent: The Kingdom Is Here," 175.

3. Hauerwas, "Repent: The Kingdom Is Here," 176.

4. Hauerwas, "Repent: The Kingdom Is Here," 176.

Rauschenbusch's social gospel theology differs greatly from Rorty's suggestions about what his grandfather argued about and envisioned for Christianity. Rorty could not and would not agree with Hauerwas's summary of his (Rorty's) grandfather's theology. Hauerwas's summary reads:

> Advocacy on its [the social gospel's] behalf consumed . . . Rauschenbusch's life. No doubt such advocacy gave Rauschenbusch . . . a sense of representing a radically different kind of Christianity. Yet they [Rauschenbusch and other social gospel advocates] remained deeply embedded in the practices of Protestant pietism. Of course the social gospel was about social reform, but it was equally about prayer, hymns, and devotional practices. The social gospel was meant to be a popular movement, and in particular a movement of the spirit . . . . "Ethics," at least the ethics of the social gospel, were as much about prayer and the singing of hymns as they were about the transformation of the economic order. More accurately put, for Rauschenbusch, the transformation of the economic order was [dependent upon] prayer.[5]

Notice that Hauerwas emphasizes Rauschenbusch's appreciation for the liturgical aspects of Christianity as much as he does the ethics that results from those practices.

What infuriates me the most about Rorty's thinking is the false dichotomy with which he continually presents Christianity and the life of the church. He writes as if Christian churches only come in two forms: *either* robustly clerical and hierarchical *or* liberal Protestant in the spirit of the social gospel. Because of this, Rorty commits the fallacy of false dichotomy when talking and writing about Christianity and the life of the church.

Additionally, his understanding of his own grandfather's social gospel theology strips away all of the interesting theological aspects of Rauschenbusch's thinking. I prefer Hauerwas's Rauschenbusch to Rorty's Rauschenbusch, but I also prefer Hauerwas's postliberal theology to Rauschenbusch's social gospel theology—which is the case whether we read Rauschenbusch on Hauerwass's theological terms or Rorty's philosophical terms. I prefer more nuanced versions of Christian churches and Christian theology than

5. Hauerwas, *A Better Hope*, 79.

Rorty, himself, depicts.[6] Whether he is *critiquing* or *defending* Christianity, Rorty maintains a fallacy of false dichotomy.[7]

With that critique of Rorty in mind, I take a warranted detour away from his predictions. Yet, this detour still relates to his set of predictions. In his most recent publication, *Minding the Web: Making Theological Connections* (2018), Hauerwas diagnoses and examines what "cracked"—importing Rorty's language into Hauerwas's book—in the 2016 presidential election.[8] Hauerwas's diagnosis involves blaming American Evangelical Christians for Trump's election, as well as offering Christians a way forward with Trump as POTUS.

Hauerwas does not call our present time the "dark years," but he helpfully and truthfully describes the acts and attitudes of cruelty that American Evangelical Christians now sign on to and support. In this regard, Hauerwas's book clearly, explicitly, and painfully identifies what the cruelties predicted by Rorty—"the gains made in the past forty years by black and brown Americans, and by homosexuals, will be wiped out," and "[j]ocular contempt for women will come back into fashion"[9]—actually look like in our current political climate.

AMERICAN EVANGELICAL CHRISTIANITY AND THE DARK YEARS

In his charitable and engaging review of *Strength of Mind*, Stephen Rankin accuses me of unfairly attacking and critiquing American Evangelical Christianity. He writes, "Goodson occasionally lapses into distracting critique and stereotype when talking about evangelical Christianity."[10] He concludes that I paint American Evangelical Christianity with "too broad a

---

6. For my full analysis of the relationship between Rauschenbusch's social gospel theology and Rorty's neo-pragmatist philosophy, see Goodson and Stone, *Introducing Prophetic Pragmatism*, ch. 2.

7. And I make this judgment after doing the most that one can to defend and understand Rorty's neo-pragmatism as an ally to Christianity—see Goodson and Stone, *Rorty and the Religious*. In that book, Stone and I encouraged scholars to find nuggets within Rorty's work that aligned with or improved upon Christianity. Importantly, Hauerwas wrote the "Foreword" to that collection of essays (see Hauerwas, "Foreword").

8. Later in this chapter, I discuss the significance of Hauerwas's title: *Minding the Web*.

9. Rorty, *AOC*, 90.

10. Rankin, Review of *Strength of Mind*, 335–37.

brushstoke."[11] Fair enough, as a critique of *Strength of Mind*. I take his critique, however, not as an invitation to leave American Evangelical Christianity alone but as an invitation to sharpen and strengthen my concerns and criticisms of currently the largest group of religious believers in the US.

In two chapters of his most recent publication, *Minding the Web*, Hauerwas mounts the strongest Christian critique—that I have read—of President Donald J. Trump and his supporters. The two chapters are entitled "The Good Life" and "Sanctuary Politics: Being the Church in the Time of Trump."[12] I present Hauerwas's arguments around the isms that Trump either benefits from or fuels: liberalism, populism, racism, sexism, and xenophobia.

In doing so, I seek to blame or to credit—whichever word a reader prefers to use—American Evangelical Christians for the election of Trump and, therefore, for potentially ushering in the "dark years."

Liberalism

In Hauerwas's judgment, liberalism is partly to blame for Trumpism. In "The Good Life," Hauerwas argues:

> Politically, liberalism increases the concentration of power in the central state, as well as at the same time underwriting the assumption of the inevitability of a globalized market. The latter has the unfortunate effect of destroying a sense of place. In such a social order, the production of wealth increasingly is in the hands of a new, rootless oligarchy "that practices a manipulative populism while holding in contempt the genuine priorities of most people." As good of a description of Trump as one could want[!][13]

According to Hauerwas, liberalism moves in two directions: while it moves inward in terms of centralizing power within a nation-state, it also moves outward in the sense that it makes a "globalized market" inevitable. This globalized market destroys "a sense of place," which many of Trump's supporters express in their own various ways, but it also allows "the production

---

11. Rankin, Review of *Strength of Mind*, 335–37.

12. The latter essay is coauthored with Hauerwas's former student, Jonathan Tran—Professor of Religion at Baylor University. References to Hauerwas, alone, signify analysis of the chapter "The Good Life"; references to Hauerwas and Tran signify analysis of the chapter "Sanctuary Politics."

13. Hauerwas, "The Good Life," 101.

of wealth" to be controlled by a "new, rootless oligarchy." Trump, himself, is part of this oligarchic class: on the one hand, he tells his supporters that he is against the globalized market; on the other hand, his anti-globalization is actually a sleight of hand because the real globalized market is controlled by Trump and those whom Trump admires (like Vladimir Putin).

Because liberalism has resulted in an oligarchic class that controls the globalized market, this means that democracy and liberalism may no longer be compatible. Hauerwas writes, "Liberalism and democracy are in tension just to the extent that liberalism can result in a populism that is indifferent to matters of truth and goodness."[14] Notice that Hauerwas does not make the typical move of blaming postmodernism for ushering in a world that is post-truth.[15] Rather, liberalism leads to indifference toward both goodness and truth. This indifference allowed for the election of Donald Trump.

Even those American conservatives who claimed to always judge politicians on the standards of goodness and truth—I am thinking, for instance, of Vice President Pence's claim made in the 1990s that one's moral character ought to be the primary factor for (s)electing a president of the United States—prioritized power over goodness and truth in the 2016 election. The word *priority*, however, might be misleading: it is not that they still work with the standards of goodness and truth and merely have lowered their standards, but they have become "indifferent to matters of truth and goodness."

As long as we continue to hold on to American forms of liberalism—which include both conservatives and liberals in the US—Hauerwas predicts that we will continue to elect dangerous politicians like Trump. Hauerwas describes our political situation in terms of the lack of truth-telling:

> For unless a people exist who have a narrative more determinative than the story shaped by the politics of the day, I fear we will continue to produce politicians like Donald Trump, people who not only seem to be dangerous but are dangerous. They are, moreover, all the more dangerous because no people seem to exist who are capable of telling them the truth.[16]

American forms of liberalism and the lack of truth-telling toward those who are dangerous politicians will mean that we are stuck with those

14. Hauerwas, "The Good Life," 108.

15. While writing the current book, this argument remained a continual temptation for me to make.

16. Hauerwas, "The Good Life," 109.

dangerous politicians. It seems that Hauerwas thinks both require change if we wish to break out of our vicious cycle: we need to exit and leave behind "the politics of the day" (liberalism), and we need truth-tellers in relation to the dangerous politicians. What will this new politics look like, and who will stand up and tell the truth to the Donald Trumps of the world?

In his typical fashion, Hauerwas addresses these questions from an unapologetically Christian perspective. He introduces his particular Christian lens in "The Good Life" but spends much more time developing a Christian critique of Trump in "Sanctuary Politics." In "The Good Life," Hauerwas writes:

> The issues surrounding the relation of Christianity and democracy will not and should not go away. The Trump campaign has raised them with new urgency. In particular, Trump has alerted us again to the worry that there is finally no check on the tyranny of the majority in democracy as we know it.[17]

Christianity becomes a critic of democracy when democracy ends up being a "tyranny of the majority." Ironically, Trump lost the majority vote in 2016 but was elected through the electoral college. I say ironically for two reasons. First, Trump's election was not the result of the "tyranny of the majority" but has resulted in a type of tyranny of a minority ruling class. Second, after the reelection of President Barack Obama, Trump tweeted on November 6, 2012: "The electoral college is a disaster for a democracy."[18]

For Hauerwas and Tran, the question is less about standing up and telling the truth to the Donald Trumps of the world and more about why Christians' voting for Trump makes the question, "What will the new politics look like?" especially urgent. In "Sanctuary Politics"—which is the phrase they give to the new politics they recommend—Hauerwas and Tran argue that, in addition to indifference toward goodness and truth, liberalism leads to a "lack of creativity":

> [A] lack of *creativity* in American politics . . . explains much of the Christian vote for Trump, which in many cases followed a form of moral reasoning that portrayed candidate Trump as . . . the only viable option. This is astounding, because there were many, many reasons why Christians should have voted otherwise—yet still many voted for Trump. If . . . 81 percent of the white evangelical

---

17. Hauerwas, "The Good Life," 110.

18. https://twitter.com/realDonaldTrump/status/266038556504494082.

vote went to Trump, then Christians basically handed Donald
Trump the presidency, even though they had every reason not to.[19]

Hauerwas and Tran make two moves here worthy of highlighting. First,
one of the problems of liberalism is that it comes with a type of determinism where citizens assume that the candidates up for election are the only
viable options for political office. This seems especially the case in relation
to the "highest" office in the land: the presidency. This determinism, which
Hauerwas and Tran identify as a "lack of creativity," means that liberalism
actually prevents true democracy because citizens assume that they must
elect whomever they are told to elect.

Second, Hauerwas and Tran focus in on American Evangelical Christians and their role in electing Trump. Contrary to their rhetoric against
liberalism, it turns out that American Evangelical Christians are the group
that embodies and embraces the politics of liberalism in the most concrete
ways. Defending and explaining that claim becomes one of the significant
tasks of Hauerwas and Tran's "Sanctuary Politics."

American Evangelical Christians embrace liberalism in the sense that
they have limited their political imagination, and their lack of political
imagination results from giving up on some of their core Christian convictions. Hauerwas and Tran claim that it "is simply not true to claim, as some
have, that Christians were forced into voting for Donald Trump. Our belief
is that believing they *had to* vote for Trump . . . followed having already
surrendered more basic Christian convictions."[20] To think that Christians
"had to vote for Trump" should always be accompanied by the recognition
that American Evangelical Christians have relinquished some of their "basic
Christian convictions." The former requires the latter: Christians voting for
Donald J. Trump becomes a possibility if and only if those Christians have
already demoted core Christian beliefs and convictions in their own lives.[21]

Furthermore, American Evangelical Christians embody liberalism in
the sense that they think of voting—rather than holding high standards
of justice—as the most important act of citizenship. Hauerwas and Tran
argue: "Christians who voted for Trump because they wanted their 'vote to
count' would have done well to remember that any politics committed to

19. Hauerwas and Tran, "Sanctuary Politics," 114.

20. Hauerwas and Tran, "Sanctuary Politics," 115.

21. Hauerwas and Tran remind American Evangelical Christians "that the possibility
of losing is no reason to give up one's commitments" (Hauerwas and Tran, "Sanctuary
Politics," 116).

justice will require great patience because unjust systems will make losing quite likely."[22] Maintaining high standards of justice, not the singular act of voting, ought to be what we consider the most important role for citizens. Liberalism, however, holds the singular act of voting in such high esteem. Embodying this aspect of liberalism, American Evangelical Christians tend to think their political obligations are fulfilled by and through going to the voting booth. (This means that it is not insignificant that Baptist and nondenominational congregations are the ones that tend to volunteer their space for voting each November.)

American Evangelical Christians embrace and embody liberalism because they fail to differentiate between America and the Christian God. Hauerwas and Tran call this failure *idolatrous*: "Christians in America . . . can no longer differentiate between America and God, something Scripture calls *idolatry* . . . which, it seems, is actually what President Trump wants of Americans."[23] Although liberalism requires a type of separation between politics and religion, liberalism also invites its citizens to think of politics as the place where salvation occurs. Secular liberalism claims that politics becomes the place where salvation occurs as a substitute for God's salvation, whereas the American Evangelical embrace of liberalism means that politics becomes the place where salvation occurs in accordance with God's purposes for salvation. Hence the American Evangelical proclamation that God "sent" Trump to "save" America,[24] which echoes Trump's own claim at the Republican National Convention in 2016 that he "alone" can save America. More than an embrace, President Trump now wants American Evangelical Christians to embody this soteriological aspect of liberalism: "what President Trump wants of Americans" is what "Scripture calls *idolatry*."[25]

---

22. Hauerwas and Tran, "Sanctuary Politics," 116.

23. Hauerwas and Tran, "Sanctuary Politics," 116.

24. Typing in "God and Trump" on Amazon.com will give readers enough material to show how strong this belief is among American Evangelical Christians, but I also cite one comment I found that provides more clarification than I wanted to have on this issue: "Scripture says God sets up kings and removes kings (Daniel 2:21). I did not think of this nor know what was going on behind the scenes among . . . evangelicals and in the heavenly realms. The book [*God and Donald Trump*] helped me realize that God actually chose Trump to be president. This is an awesome thought. We must pray for him and support him and vote for him again in 2020" (five-star review of *God and Donald Trump* by Dottie Parish, Nov 27, 2018, Amazon.com).

25. Hauerwas and Tran, "Sanctuary Politics," 116.

Populism

In an illuminating section called "Populism, Elitism, and Fear," Hauerwas and Tran argue that we need to delineate between "two kinds of fear operating around Trump's presidency." The first "is the fear that drove some to vote for candidate Trump even when there were plenty of reasons and ways not to do so," and the second "is the fear that surfaced in response to his candidacy, a fear that has publicly intensified during, and . . . because of, his presidency."[26] Hauerwas and Tran's point is that both Trump's supporters and detractors are driven by fear; I would add to this that Trump, himself, feeds off of both "kinds of fear."

These differing fears lead to odd affiliations and divisions. Hauerwas and Tran talk about that oddness by contrasting "identity politics" with their use of "sanctuary politics":

> The presumption that white elites share common cause with the white underclass just because they are white shows just how unhelpful American identity politics can be, as tortured as the accompanying belief that poor whites and poor ethnic minorities share little in common. Poverty, to be sure, disproportionately affects minorities and women, yet poverty in America is a persistently pervasive enough phenomenon that there remains plenty in which to share. Insofar as it breaks down, divisions erected by Trump's parroted identity politics, sanctuary politics avails shared life, including life shared over against the disproportions . . . that would otherwise make the gathered enemies of another.[27]

Identity politics, both in its liberal and Trumpist versions, turns neighbors into enemies because it encourages unnecessary divisions and forges partnerships on the most shallow standard possible: the whiteness of one's skin. (Of course, we ought to note how this differs from Rorty's attempt to turn strangers into neighbors.) Hauerwas and Tran instead defend "sanctuary politics"—which "avails shared life" together, "including life shared over against the disproportions."[28]

In the end, identity politics—again, both in its liberal and Trumpist versions—neglects the poor. In what is perhaps the best single sentence of the book, Hauerwas and Tran write: "[I]dentity politics [leads to] a junk

---

26. Hauerwas and Tran, "Sanctuary Politics," 118.

27. Hauerwas and Tran, "Sanctuary Politics," 123–24.

28. Hauerwas and Tran, "Sanctuary Politics," 124.

populism that further robs the poor."[29] The populism that led to Trump's election, and the populism we continue to live with and tolerate, is best described as a "junk populism" because the poor continue to be the real victims and remain neglected. The poor might have voted for Trump, but Trump's presidency makes life harder for the poor. To play off a classical story: under Trump and within our globalized oligarchy, the American system now more explicitly robs from the poor and gives to the rich.

Racism

Although Trump's racism has been a fact about him for quite some time, Hauerwas observes that he revealed it most concretely during his presidential campaign when claiming to be the "law and order" candidate.[30] While Trump's racism is a deep problem, Hauerwas argues that it actually represents a "deeper pathology" within American life:

> Yet the racism and fear Trump uses to give the impression that he would be a "strong leader" are, I believe, manifestations of an even deeper pathology—namely, the profound sense of unease that many Americans have about their lives. That unease often takes the form of resentment against elites, but, even more troubling, it funds the prejudice against minority groups . . . . Resentment is another word for the unease that seems to grip many good, middle-class—mostly white—people.[31]

In short, racism in America results from prejudice and resentment. This argument can be translated as the first of two mathematical-political formulas that can be abstracted from Hauerwas's *Minding the Web*:

prejudice + resentment = racism

Hauerwas also reflects on the role of anger within racism:

> [M]any Americans are angry, but they are not sure towards whom that anger is appropriately directed. Their anger needs direction, and Trump is more than happy to tell Americans—particularly if they are white—who their enemy is, as well as whom they should hate. There is a therapeutic aspect to Trump's rhetoric because

29. Hauerwas and Tran, "Sanctuary Politics," 125.

30. "Trump's claim to restore law and order ignores the racist presumption that gave birth to the phrase in the first place" (Hauerwas, "The Good Life," 97).

31. Hauerwas, *Minding the Web*, 97.

he gives people an enemy that delays any acknowledgement that those with whom they should be angry may be themselves.[32]

Angry, prejudiced, resentful white people needed to know who they should be angry and resentful *toward*: these are the people who supported and voted for Donald Trump because he "is more than happy to tell [them] who their enemy is, as well as whom they should hate." Racism, itself, is a problem—what Hauerwas calls a "sin" of white Americans throughout the book. However, racism points toward another problem as well: the anger, hatred, and resentment directed toward minorities "gives people an enemy that delays any acknowledgement that those with whom they should be angry" are themselves.

When my children were younger and still threw temper tantrums but also had a vocabulary to communicate and express their feelings, my strategy with them would be to let them get their anger and frustrations out and then raise the question, "Can you use your words to tell me what it is you actually want?" It seems like we are in a similar situation with those who voted for and support Trump! Although on Twitter he acts like he lost the election, Trump won; so the tantrum(s) should be over. Now, the questions become: What kind of society do these angry, hateful, resentful white Americans actually want? What does the "again," in "Make America Great Again" (MAGA), actually refer to? For what are Trump and these white Americans nostalgic?

I have yet to read or hear any persuasive answers to this set of questions until Hauerwas's *Minding the Web*. In my judgment, Hauerwas and Tran give a persuasive answer to this set of questions:

> [W]hen its antidote to global capitalism turns out to be the establishment of a 1950s version of Judeo-Christian Victorian society, without the recognition of that culture's stewardship of capitalism or America's guiding role of its operations, then its nationalism turns out to be only . . . the most nostalgic kind: to make America white again. The end result will be a nationalist-because-anti-globalist agenda that can achieve little more than a protectionist version of capitalism and a pseudo-intellectual endorsement of white supremacist activity. Not particularly original but highly dangerous.[33]

---

32. Hauerwas, *Minding the Web*, 98.

33. Hauerwas and Tran, "Sanctuary Politics," 120.

Hauerwas and Tran display a "courage to truth" here concerning those in power—Trump and his Republican colleagues—and those who support Trump and his rhetoric.[34] What they want, without explicitly saying it, is "to make America white again." Of course, America was never "white." For this to be one's desire means that one wants to return to the enslavement of African Americans and the genocide of Native Americans—perhaps not the exact forms of genocide and slavery as they were performed in American history, but new ways to enslave and execute non-white American citizens?

The ultimate vision of Trump and his supporters is for America to be more insular, more "white," and wealthier on capitalist standards. This vision is neither interesting nor original "but highly dangerous."[35] Because of its shallowness and superficiality, uneducated white Americans buy in to it.

Xenophobia

Of course, populism and racism become so interconnected in the American context that it becomes intellectually irresponsible to treat populism as its own phenomenon. Hauerwas and Tran connect the two with clarity and insight:

> Trump's entry into America's longstanding class war comes in his ability to appropriate a populist agenda and politically manipulate it to elitist ends . . . . Rather than help the white underclass ferret out any associated racism . . . , Trump fans the racism and exasperates the conditions that in turn exasperates the racism. We can understand the rise in brazen hate crimes across America as enabled by Trump, and the brazenness itself as something he emboldened. The conditions that make for this strain of racism . . . are the many excesses of capitalism riding roughshod over the local ecologies that poor folks call home.[36]

Since Trump has the attention and respect of the "white underclass," Hauerwas and Tran make the remarkable—almost unbelievable—suggestion that he could have helped "ferret out" racism. What a world that would be! Obviously, that is not what has happened. Rather, "Trump fans the racism" and enables "brazen hate crimes across America."

34. On the phrase "courage to truth," see Michel Foucault's *Courage to Truth*. For my adoption of Foucault's argument as a pedagogical guide, see Goodson, *SM*, ch. 7.

35. Hauerwas and Tran, "Sanctuary Politics," 120.

36. Hauerwas and Tran, "Sanctuary Politics," 120.

Hauerwas and Tran also focus on the conditions that make Trump's "populist agenda" possible. Such conditions are the result of "the many excesses of capitalism," which have destroyed the "local ecologies"—the communities and towns—that "poor [white] folks call home." Hauerwas and Tran suggest that capitalism, not immigrants, should be considered the proper object of blame for the conditions that have made life difficult for "poor [white] folks."[37] Trump benefits too much from capitalism for him to be truthful about the real cause of the struggles "poor [white] folks" face, and for some reason the "poor [white] folks" buy into Trump making immigrants the object of blame—even if they find themselves in a community or town where immigrants actually help the economy a great deal.

What we have, therefore, is another—a second—type of mathematical-political formula that defines and describes where we find ourselves today:

populism + racism = xenophobia

This formula is helpful, but only because it depicts how the blame gets misplaced. The "excesses of capitalism" ought to be blamed for the struggles "poor [white] folks" face.

Hauerwas and Tran conclude their reflections on Trump by making three strong arguments about how Christians are behaving vs. how they ought to behave during the Trump presidency. First, Christians "will continue in a faith emptied of everything but the luxuries of privilege." Hauerwas and Tran continue, "If they persist with their [American] myths and [political] accommodations, then they will continue self-righteously dumbstruck in the face of eventualities like the election of Donald Trump."[38]

Second, Hauerwas and Tran plumb the depths of Christian beliefs to make a case for why and when American Christians ought to start identifying as Muslims:

> If the Trump administration should follow its brinksmanship logic and begin forcibly to register Muslims, Christians might identify as Muslims—something God in God's extravagance did in identifying with creation, for the sake of creation, and something Christians in their closefisted self-regard failed to do with Jews under the Third Reich.[39]

---

37. I use the word "difficult" quite deliberately—as in how the "difficulty of reality" presents itself in the twenty-first century; see Goodson, *SM*, ch. 8.

38. Hauerwas and Tran, "Sanctuary Politics," 121.

39. Hauerwas and Tran, "Sanctuary Politics," 123.

While it seems unlikely that such a registry will occur during Trump's first term, his reelection might empower him to make such a move in his second term. If that happens, then Christians ought to "identify as Muslim." Hauerwas and Tran's reason for this is not in terms of being a "good liberal"; rather, the reason they present is a deeply theological one: this is analogous to what God did/does for gentiles. Additionally, Christians should not fail at doing this once more since Christians failed at this task during German Nazism. Then, Christians should have registered themselves as Jews; now, if Trump forces a Muslim registry, Christians should register themselves as Muslims.

Third, Hauerwas and Tran argue that Christians who support Trump might "have forgotten what it means to be Christian" in relation to Christian beliefs about immigration:

> Shockingly, there remain to this day Christians who support Trump's anti-migration policies because they believe his policies will "keep us safe." Surely, one could not wish for a more misleading understanding of what it means to be Christian. Christians worship at the church of martyrs; they seek fellowship with the crucified Lord. Being a Christian is not about being safe, but about challenging the status quo in ways that cannot help but put you in danger. Thinking it possible to be safe in a world where Christians are sent out like sheep among wolves . . . [means] that those Christians who voted for Trump because of his willingness to use questionable tactics to keep them safe have forgotten what it means to be Christian.[40]

Notice two significant moves here: (a) the problem of xenophobia is that it misplaces the need for safety and security within the Christian life, and (b) xenophobia does not mean that one ceases to be a true Christian but, rather, that one forgets "what it means to be Christian."

I wish to linger on this latter point. Its importance cannot be overstated because of how debates on social media tend to go. Debates and discussions on social media usually include Christians on the Left saying that those who support Trump's immigration policies are no longer Christian—as if taking a position within American politics can negate one's Christian salvation. (Of course, Christians on the Right do the same to those Christians who support *Roe v. Wade*, etc.) With their shift to the role of memory, Hauerwas and Tran model a better way for Christians to disagree during a

---

40. Hauerwas and Tran, "Sanctuary Politics," 124–25.

time of such political divisiveness. Christians do not cease being Christian because of their racism, xenophobia, and/or support for Donald Trump; rather, Christians become *forgetful* about "what it means to be Christian" if they are racist, xenophobic, and support Trump's policies on immigration.

Sexism

According to Hauerwas and Tran, sexism ought to be judged as "the most tragic result . . . of Christians [voting] for Trump." What do they mean by this judgment? They argue:

> [T]he most tragic result . . . of Christians having voted for Trump in order . . . to secure his support on the issue of abortion is this: women in America have long worried that Christian pro-life arguments objectify them, reducing them to bodies and glossing over the myriad complexities women face in all aspects of contemporary life. After pro-life Christians voted into the White House a person who actually *does* . . . objectify women, their nightmares about Christians appear to have been realized . . . . [W]e find it telling that much of the church championed a candidate accused of behavior that cannot but endorse those most culpably associated with abortion—namely, men who refuse to take responsibility for their actions. The 2016 election . . . demonstrated how many Christians remain unable to separate their pro-life stance from their misogyny and how willing they are to abdicate Christian witness in order to win a culture war no one else seems to be fighting. All this will prove a deal with the devil for which Christian evangelistic efforts will surely pay.[41]

Character matters. Character matters in terms of the debate on abortion. Character matters in terms of men taking "responsibility for their actions" toward women.

If so-called pro-life Christians want to convince American society that abortions are intrinsically wrongful acts, then they have worsened their pro-life position by using abortion as justification for voting for Donald Trump. If there is an object worthy of blame for women needing abortions, then Trump's character represents that object of blame. Both the objectification of women and men's refusal "to take responsibility for their actions"

---

41. Hauerwas and Tran, "Sanctuary Politics," 117.

should be what pro-life Christians focus their attention on. Otherwise, pro-life Christianity becomes merely a baptized misogyny.[42]

Hauerwas and Tran are deeply and painfully right about the misogyny of current pro-life Christianity. Given the culmination of these arguments about and against American Evangelical Christians and their support for President Trump, do we now have even more reason for despair concerning the "dark years"? Hauerwas's title signals how to negate this question.

MINDING THE WEB

Exploring the significance of the title of Hauerwas's book *Minding the Web: Making Theological Connections* becomes a necessary task because such an analysis reveals how Hauerwas's postliberalism leads to hopefulness—instead of cynicism, despair, and/or hopelessness—during the "dark years." For Hauerwas, hope can be found in some of the forgotten and neglected beliefs of Christianity.

Hauerwas's use of the word web contains family resemblances with the American philosopher and Harvard professor W. V. O. Quine's epistemological argument known as the "web of belief." According to Quine, "Beliefs typically rest . . . on further beliefs" where some "of the . . . supporting beliefs may record the reports of observations, but often in making a belief acceptable to someone there is no need to cite observations" because the "person [or people] may already share enough of the other supporting beliefs so that merely calling attention to some of the relevant connections will suffice."[43] According to Quine, the web works in this way:

> We convince someone of something by appealing to beliefs he already holds and by combining these to induce further beliefs in him, step by step, until the belief we wanted finally to inculcate in him is inculcated. The most striking examples of such arguments, no doubt, are mathematical. The beliefs we invoke at the beginning of such an argument may be self-evident truths: this was Euclid's way. But they need not be, so long they are beliefs our friend already holds.[44]

---

42. My understanding of misogyny has been deeply shaped by Kate Manne's *Down Girl: The Logic of Misogyny*.

43. Quine and Ullian, *The Web of Belief*, 76.

44. Quine and Ullian, *The Web of Belief*, 77.

Quine's explanation for how this "web" works matches up quite well with how Hauerwas speaks to American Evangelical Christians in *Minding the Web*.

Christians who support Trump, Hauerwas claims, have forgotten what it means to be Christian—which means that Hauerwas *reasons with* American Evangelical Christians on the terms of Quine's "web of belief":

> To convince someone of something we work back to beliefs he already holds and argue from them as premises. Perhaps we also insinuate some supporting beliefs, as needed further premises. We may succeed in insinuating a supporting belief simply by stating it, or we may be called on to offer support for it in turn. We aim, of course, for supporting beliefs that the person is readier to adopt than the thing we are trying finally to convince him of. His readiness to adopt what we put to him will depend partly on its intrinsic plausibility and partly on his confidence in us.[45]

In *Minding the Web*, Hauerwas successfully minds the web of Christian beliefs in order to help American Evangelical Christians remember the significant beliefs and premises of the Christian faith.

The word minding suggests an active use of the intellect, and—given Hauerwas's role in the return to virtue theory in the academy—this active use might be best expressed in terms of cultivating and displaying intellectual virtue. As we often find in Hauerwas's books, he lays out both the condition for virtue as well as his recommendations for which virtues need to be cultivated and displayed given the context and problems in which Christians find themselves. Because of the use of the word "minding," I interpret Hauerwas's *Minding the Web* as his most extensive treatment of *intellectual* virtue.

In terms of the condition for intellectual virtue, Hauerwas says quite clearly that such a condition involves recognizing "our dependency on the other." This recognition is not a virtue itself but, rather, a condition for virtue. What does Hauerwas mean by this? He answers, "[O]ur dependency on the other is the resource that makes possible the acquisition of the virtues necessary for the good *working of our reason*."[46] Because of this final phrase, "the good working of our reason," I feel confident interpreting Hauerwas's *Minding the Web* as his most extensive treatment of the intellectual virtues—which turns out to be quite helpful for articulating how

---

45. Quine and Ullian, *The Web of Belief*, 78.
46. Hauerwas, *Minding the Web*, 56; emphasis added.

Christians might learn to move on after the American Evangelical support of Donald J. Trump.

Hauerwas clarifies his use of "dependency on the other": "[T]he recognition of our dependence on one another is a resource for the possibility of recognition across traditions. Such recognition . . . depend[s] on the ability to acknowledge our lack of self-knowledge."[47] What does this lack of self-knowledge result from? Hauerwas claims that it "is the result of our failure to recognize our dependency on others."[48] If we are in the "dark years," as Rorty claims we are, then forging a different and new future for ourselves involves making the recognition of our dependence on others part of the conditions for living and thinking.

The intellectual virtues recommended by Hauerwas in *Minding the Web* include humility, hope, insight, listening, and love. By humility as an intellectual virtue, Hauerwas makes a surprising recommendation: "[P]ride and humility 'come in handy' when . . . engaged in prolonged and difficult tasks" because the proper amount of pride fends off "practicing false humility," while true humility serves as a constant reminder that others might speak and think (and, since it's 2020, tweet) in ways "greater than [our] own."[49]

Saving hope and love for last, what does Hauerwas mean by insight and listening as intellectual virtues? By insight, Hauerwas means a type of self-awareness. He argues that some critics of his think that his "emphasis on the importance of the virtues [is] a distraction" to the theological task, but Hauerwas finds that emphasizing the virtues leads to better "insight about the human condition": "The virtues reside in wisdom traditions because they require insight about the human condition."[50] Hauerwas also shifts from the general category of "the human condition" to the particularity of the individual and, hence, self-awareness when he argues that what seems "absent" among those men who sexually abuse others is "psychological insight."[51]

---

47. Hauerwas, *Minding the Web*, 56.

48. Hauerwas, *Minding the Web*, 56.

49. Hauerwas, *Minding the Web*, 29. I have totally ignored the context in my presentation of Hauerwas's reflections on humility as an intellectual virtue. The context involves Hauerwas praising the author Craig Keen for admitting and balancing "pride and humility" in talking about Keen's own book: *After Crucifixion: The Promise of Theology*.

50. Hauerwas, *Minding the Web*, 153.

51. See Hauerwas, *Minding the Web*, 151–52. Again, I am neglecting the context: this is Hauerwas's essay reflecting upon his friendship with John Howard Yoder—whom we now know sexually assaulted and harassed several of his female students.

Listening as an intellectual virtue does not differ that much from insight as an intellectul virtue, but Hauerwas's emphases within each differ. By listening, Hauerwas means the "hard discipline . . . [t]o learn first to be silent." He adds that listening, as an intellectual virtue, "threatens" our need for "control" and tests our desire "to anticipate what you are going to say, prior to what you say, so I can respond before you have said anything."[52] Hauerwas hits the nail on the head for how dominant intellectual vice is in our current political climate: neither Democrat nor Republican displays the ability to listen to one another on each other's terms. Rather, both Democrats and Republicans dismiss one another prior to listening and understanding each other.

Hope and love are the two virtues that have received the most attention in the present book. Similar to my own argument about hope in *Strength of Mind*, where I define hope as "the realistic, reasonable, and virtuous way to use one's imagination,"[53] Hauerwas strongly distinguishes between hope and optimism—concluding that "an optimistic hope will . . . not sustain you from one episode to the next."[54] Hope differs from optimism, but

> it is also the case that you cannot survive without hope, though a hope that is grounded in a very different reality than optimism. The kind of hope that sustains you is a hope that makes endurance an ongoing way of life without the refusal to give up destroying you. Such a hope takes the form of prayer, in which God is made present in the lives of those suffering from a debilitating illness, as well as those that care for them. In short, hope is a virtue that sustains with the conviction that no life is without meaning.[55]

As an intellectual virtue, hope "sustains . . . the conviction that no life is without meaning." As a virtue, hope achieves a golden mean between the extremes of optimism and nihilism—the assumption or belief that life has no meaning. This golden mean becomes necessary in the "dark years" because, I argue, *an unrealistic optimism remains a real temptation among the Left and versions of complete nihilism have come to dominate extremes on the Right.* This is one of the primary claims and warnings of the present book:

---

52. Hauerwas, *Minding the Web*, 174.

53. Goodson, *SM*, 210.

54. Hauerwas, *Minding the Web*, 140.

55. Hauerwas, *Minding the Web*, 140.

citizens must begin working hard to find this particular golden mean between nihilism and optimism—a golden mean best called hope.[56]

For Hauerwas, love is an intellectual virtue that moderates how we relate to those who differ from us. Hauerwas writes, "If love . . . is [defined as] the nonviolent apprehension of the other as other, then you cannot love everyone in general."[57] However, the "love that matters is that which does not fear difference."[58] Hauerwas concludes that Christians are obligated "to love one another" (other Christians) and to love those whom they fear.[59] In his defense of why Christians are obligated to love those whom they fear, he connects love with hope: given "that we live in a dangerous world in which reliance on those who promise safety only makes the world more dangerous," Christians ought "to prepare their hearts and minds for receiving the . . . love [that] transforms our fears [in]to hope."[60] To love others means loving others whom we fear; when this type of love occurs, it means that our fear has been transformed into hope. My primary claim in this part of the book concerns how American Evangelical Christians have given up on the virtue of love, and Hauerwas's argument leads to the conclusion that *giving up on love as a virtue also entails the failure to cultivate hope.*

PEDAGOGICAL HOPE, POSTLIBERALISM, AND POVERTY

In two essays prior to the publication of *Minding the Web*, Stanley Hauerwas offers what I consider a postliberal account of charity, friendship, and poverty. In this section, I analyze his account and the arguments that accompany it in order to build a case for what I call pedagogical hope. If we are indeed in the "dark years," then professors and scholars need to learn to teach and write with pedagogical hope.

Philosophy, Politics, and the Poor

According to Hauerwas, teaching philosophy necessarily involves a political task. This task relates to the poor, to those who live in poverty. Building

56. On how to apply to the logic of the golden mean to hope, see Goodson and Stone's *Introducing Prophetic Pragmatism*, ch. 5, and Goodson's *SM*, ch. 8.

57. Hauerwas, *Minding the Web*, 172.

58. Hauerwas, *Minding the Web*, 172.

59. See Hauerwas, *Minding the Web*, 172, 243–44.

60. Hauerwas, *Minding the Web*, 244.

from "the philosophical rhetorician"[61] Gregory of Nazianzus's (329–390 C.E.) "On Love for the Poor," Hauerwas argues that philosophers have an obligation "to make the poor seen" through what we teach and write.[62] This political task comes with the insight that all of us are "subject to fickle fortune," which means that we help readers and students see "that those who are better off should never be tempted to think that because they are so they are fundamentally different than the poor."[63]

Gregory of Nazianzus serves as a model for this work, not only through his "On Love for the Poor," but also in his own life. Hauerwas explains:

> Gregory . . . received the best education available, but that education had not alienated him from the poor. Yet that is exactly what happens to most that receive university education in our time. At best, the modern university produces people, even some who may have come to the university from poverty, who after being at the university want to "do something for the poor." The university is not able to produce people, as Gregory was able, to see and describe the poor as beautiful. He was able to see the beauty of the poor [and] had no reason to deny or wish they did not exist.[64]

Hauerwas's interweaving of Gregory's lack of alienation from the poor with the failures of the modern university becomes extremely useful for thinking about what philosophy can and should achieve post–academic McCarthyism *and* post-neoliberalism (postliberalism, for short).

In the modern university, philosophy has bought in to (pun intended) the presuppositions of Western capitalism—that *overcoming* poverty leads to gaining ethical, political, and social agency—over those of philosophical arguments concerning fortune and luck. Of course, this is a lie. Although it may seem odd to enlist the aristocratic Aristotle in this argument, in *Poetics* he introduces the notion that we come to see different classes through various aesthetic categories. While I disagree with his claim that those without power can be seen only in the aesthetic category of comedy, Aristotle's *Poetics* offers a philosophical starting point for making sense of Hauerwas's claim that we ought to teach our students "to see and describe the poor

---

61. Hauerwas claims that Frederick Norris is the first to identify Gregory of Nazianzus as a "philosophical rhetorician"—a description that Hauerwas seems to fully embrace in his exposition of Gregory of Nazianzus's arguments concerning the poor.

62. Hauerwas uses this phrase throughout *The State of the University*, 187–201.

63. Hauerwas, *State of the University*, 193.

64. Hauerwas, *State of the University*, 198.

as beautiful." At the very least, philosophers ought to challenge standard assumptions about and prejudices against the unemployed and the working poor that students bring with them to their undergraduate education—which also might be reinforced in their other collegiate courses. In short, philosophers need to teach and write in ways that invite our students and readers to "see" the poor as beautiful.

Remembering the Poor

The essay "How to 'Remember the Poor'" serves as Hauerwas's sequel to "To Love God, the Poor, and Learning." Hauerwas claims that "How to 'Remember the Poor'" is simply a commentary—in essay form—on the verse, from the Christian canon, Galatians 2:10: "They asked only one thing, that we remember the poor, which actually is what I was eager to do." My claim is that because of academic McCarthyism and neoliberalism, the second chapter of Galatians ought to be added and read alongside Rorty's interpretation of 1 Corinthians 13.

Interestingly, Hauerwas begins his essay with a negative judgment on his own writing career—a negative judgment that fits precisely into the historical narrative constructed and defended in chapter 1 of the present book. Hauerwas confesses,

> One of the reasons I am intent to address questions surrounding what it means to remember the poor, or . . . why charity is at the heart of Christian living, is that I do not think I have adequately dealt with the challenge [of what it means to] be a community of the poor that cares for the poor.[65]

This confession should not surprise my readers. On the terms of the timeline that I constructed in chapter 1, Hauerwas's formation as a scholar must have been impacted by academic McCarthyism. From the 1950s to 1970s, scholars did not "adequately deal . . . with the challenge[s]" of the unemployed and working poor in this country. With the rise of identity politics in the 1980s and 1990s, the unemployed and working poor continued to be neglected by professors and scholars. Hauerwas's confession represents a general problem within the American academy, not only his own particular habits and interests.

---

65. Hauerwas, *The Work of Theology*, 209.

After offering this confession, Hauerwas's argument proceeds in the following way: first, with an explanation concerning why charity ought to be considered an obligation; second, with an account of the problem of "charity in the world of capitalism"; and third, with "a plea for charity" toward the poor in the twenty-first-century university. I build my argument from each of these points.

Hauerwas surprisingly categorizes charity as an obligation, instead of as a virtue, and claims that this obligation extends to all citizens—even to those who live in poverty. How can the poor fulfill their obligation to be charitable? Hauerwas recommends charity through friendship: "To be poor does not mean you lack the means to extend charity to another. You may lack money or food but you have the gift of friendship to overwhelm the loneliness that grips the lives of so many."[66] The poor can fulfill their obligation of charity through friendship with those who are gripped by loneliness.

The inference I make from Hauerwas's argument allows me to introduce a key phrase for the overall argument of this book: *pedagogical hope.* If these are the "dark years," then professors and scholars have an obligation to teach and write with pedagogical hope. In relation to Hauerwas's argument: teaching and writing with pedagogical hope entails helping our readers and students understand how friendship can become an act of charity toward those who experience cruelty, humiliation, loneliness, shame, and unintended solitude.

What does charity look like in the "world of capitalism"? To answer this question, Hauerwas provides a lengthy genealogy of the role of beggars and the poor within different theories of capitalism. His genealogy runs as follows.

The founder of Western capitalism, Adam Smith, distinguishes between beggars and the poor. In Hauerwas's words:

> Smith distinguished . . . between the poor and beggars. The poor could be subject to our sympathy as long as they sought to be like those who were not poor. Yet it was Smith's hope that capitalism as a system for the production of wealth would provide an alternative that would eliminate poverty. Indeed one way to think of Smith's vision is to see capitalism itself as a system of charity. No longer will individual acts of charity be required, because the system itself

66. Hauerwas, *The Work of Theology*, 214.

will raise all the boats as the water rises. Capitalism so understood
is an extraordinary utopian project.[67]

For Smith, the poor earn the sympathy of others by acting like they are
not poor. Beggars do not earn the sympathy of others. Smith's theory of
capitalism promises the end of poverty. Because of this promise, Smith sees
capitalism as an institutional and systematic form of charity toward the
poor. Smith's theory of capitalism renders individual acts of charity toward
the poor unnecessary whereas beggars remain underserving of individual
acts of charity.

Following Smith's theory of capitalism, Hauerwas actually treats Walter Rauschenbusch's social gospel theology as a response to and its own
theory of capitalism. According to Hauerwas, Rauschenbusch takes Adam
Smith up on his proposal that capitalism institutionalizes and systematizes
charity—which no longer makes charity the obligation of individual citizens. For Rauschenbusch, and *contra* the reasoning found in 1 Corinthians
13, justice replaces charity as the most important virtue for Christian dis-
cipleship.[68] In this sense, Rorty's notions of solidarity and sympathy—to
the extent that they are his versions of justice—follow his maternal grandfather's thinking more closely than his (Rorty's) defense of charity and love
do in his turn to 1 Corinthians 13.

Next, Hauerwas argues that Reinhold Niebuhr continues the substitu-
tion of charity with justice. "For Niebuhr," Hauerwas claims, "the only way
to do something substantive about poverty was to use the technologies of
power available to the dispossessed to challenge the often-hidden power of
the established order."[69] Niebuhr's justice-centered reasoning shifted the
whole enterprise of Christian ethics from thinking in terms of individual
acts of charity to resolving that charity ought to be left up to political and
social policy. Hauerwas credits Niebuhr with changing "the world in terms
of how Christians—particularly in America—understood how the poor
were to be served."[70] Rather "than focusing on individual acts of charity,
Christians now tried to imagine social policies that would make the poor
no longer poor."[71] Hauerwas continues with an ironic praise of "Niebuhr's

67. Hauerwas, *The Work of Theology*, 221.

68. See Hauerwas, *The Work of Theology*, 222.

69. Hauerwas, *The Work of Theology*, 223.

70. Hauerwas, *The Work of Theology*, 223.

71. Hauerwas, *The Work of Theology*, 223.

extraordinary ability to imagine and support policies that offered some care for the poor."[72]

Adam Smith originated the notion that capitalism would rid the world of the poor; Walter Rauschenbusch bought in to this notion and implemented a shift from charity to justice; and Reinhold Niebuhr ran with this notion and reimagined Christian ethics based upon how the poor are not the responsibility of individual citizens but the responsibility of a centralized power—located in both the free-market and the nation-state.

The final part of Hauerwas's genealogy focuses on the American Democratic Party of the late twentieth and early twenty-first centuries. Under the influence of Niebuhr's political philosophy, American Christians "became more concerned with trying to make the government the agent [that] cares for the poor rather than [following the verse in Galatians to] 'remember the poor.'"[73] This concern found a home in the Democratic Party of the United States of America in the sense that American "Christians increasingly came to believe that their obligation to care about the poor could be met by voting for the left wing of the Democratic Party—a vain ambition given the fact that there is now no left wing of the Democratic Party."[74] Hauerwas's genealogy ends with the observation that American Christians assume that charity is now the work of the Democratic Party, and poverty will come to an end once capitalism is allowed to fulfill its promises to all citizens. The Right thinks that free-market capitalism will solve the problem of poverty whereas the Left thinks that the government will solve the problem of poverty.

On the terms of the present book, Hauerwas's genealogy represents the background to neoliberalism. The assumption and promise that poverty will come to an end once capitalism is allowed to fulfill its promises to all citizens becomes a primary piece of neoliberalism. This is a faulty assumption and a false promise, and the end of neoliberalism means the acceptance and acknowledgment that capitalism has not brought about an end to poverty. The academic Left has neglected this fact, and the unemployed and working poor understandably looked toward a "strongman" to serve as a response to these broken promises.

---

72. Hauerwas, *The Work of Theology*, 223.

73. Hauerwas, *The Work of Theology*, 224.

74. Hauerwas, *The Work of Theology*, 224.

Under neoliberalism, the poor become an enemy.[75] Neoliberalism makes poverty a problem to solve—indeed, another "them" to eliminate through political and social policies—rather than persons to befriend and love. When the problem remains, the poor become an "enemy" because they signify a kind of proof that capitalism fails on its big promises.

What I have been calling Hauerwas's postliberalism concerns the connections he makes between charity, friendship, and the poor. He writes with eloquence about these connections:

> [W]e need to know how to be with the poor in such a manner that the gifts the poor receive do not make impossible friendship between the giver and the recipient . . . . I do not mean to suggest that friendship is some kind of magical relation that will make the dependencies associated with aid less likely. Friendships, at least superficial friendships, are just as likely to produce dependency as direct aid . . . . [G]enuine friendship depends on people being truthful with one another . . . There is no substitute for people being honest.[76]

Although Rorty claims that philosophy fails to account for friendship, I argue that philosophers in the twenty-first century need to prove Rorty wrong—and in radical ways. The task of philosophy in the twenty-first century involves offering wisdom for our readers and students to learn to be *with the poor, to think and act for the poor,* and *to share community with the poor.*

Forging these connections between charity, friendship, and the poor are some of the most important tasks for philosophers in the twenty-first century. Friendships with those living in poverty escape the limitations put on friendship(s) under and within neoliberalism because friendships with the unemployed and working poor can be neither controlled by nor reduced to economic purposes. If philosophers avoid this task, then we display hopelessness toward all citizens in society. If philosophers avoid this task, then we fail our discipline (in its Socratic form), our readers, and our students. If philosophers avoid this task, we teach and write without pedagogical hope toward our readers and students.

---

75. In Hauerwas's words, "But I fear too often the attempt to defeat an enemy may make us a mirror image of what we oppose" (Hauerwas, *The Work of Theology*, 225).

76. Hauerwas, *The Work of Theology*, 226.

Pedagogical Hope

Pedagogical hope relates to what I defend and describe as intellectual hope in *Strength of Mind*. In *Strength of Mind*, I conclude chapter 8 with these words:

> I define intellectual hope as the realistic, reasonable, and virtuous way to use one's imagination . . . . The word "realistic" prevents hope from becoming mere optimism. The word "reasonable" highlights the necessary role of the intellect for learning to become hopeful. The word "virtuous" emphasizes the logic of the golden mean for thinking about hope and the need to avoid extremes in our hopefulness. Intellectual hope offers a bigger umbrella than imaginative hope. Intellectual hope incorporates imaginative hope because it includes the faculty of the imagination, but imaginative hope does not necessarily involve intellectual hope . . . . The imagination serves us well when and only when we use it realistically, reasonably, and virtuously. If we continually and constantly use the faculty of the imagination in these ways, then we . . . cultivate . . . intellectual hope.[77]

Pedagogical hope relates to intellectual hope in the sense that it identifies the *process* of cultivating "the realistic, reasonable, and virtuous way[s] to use one's imagination." The work of philosophy, perhaps the most important work philosophers have in the twenty-first century, involves teaching with pedagogical hope. If we experience thirty years of darkness, then we must increase and intensify pedagogical hope within our teaching and writing. The "dark years" become *more* of a reason, not less of one, to cultivate hopefulness through our teaching and writing.

CONCLUSIONS

Coming full circle in this chapter, Hauerwas claims that American Evangelical Christianity has made a "deal with the devil" by voting for Donald Trump and supporting Trump's presidency.[78] *On both Paul's and Richard Rorty's terms, American Evangelical Christians exhibit faith with neither hope nor love.*

---

77. Goodson, *SM*, 210–11.

78. See Hauerwas, *Minding the Web*, 117.

Earlier in this book, I raised the question: when will American Evangelical Christians—who claim to read Paul's epistles literally—catch on to the language and logic of 1 Corinthians 13 and catch up to Rorty's Christian love ethic? Hauerwas's arguments in *Minding the Web* lead us to a similar question: when will Christians in America "mind the web"—explore the depths—of their Christian faith and believe in the full promises of Pauline Christianity? When will Christians in America give up on hate—hatred that I have been nicely calling racism, sexism, and xenophobia in this chapter—and embody the charity and love described by Paul that comes to them as a gift of the Holy Spirit? When will Christians realize that the gifts of the Holy Spirit, on the terms of their own theological reasoning, supply them with what they need economically, politically, and socially—not only spiritually and theologically? *Minding the Web* represents a book that had to be written, after 2016, partly because of Hauerwas's clear and wise diagnosis of Christianity during this time of Trump's presidency but mostly because he calls and reminds Christians to mind their own web of beliefs and stop thinking that the American Republican Party will "save" Christians and "save" Christianity.[79]

Returning to Martin Heidegger's thinking as a way to conclude this particular chapter: perhaps we are at a time in American history, what Rorty rightly or wrongly calls the "dark years," where we need to be reminded of the truth found in Heidegger's words of lament, "*Only . . . God can save us now.*"[80]

---

79. Significantly, the title of Hauerwas's essay on Walter Rauschenbusch in *A Better Hope* is "Walter Rauschenbusch and the Saving of America."

80. Heidegger, "'Only a God Can Save Us'"; emphasis added.

Conclusion

Failed Pragmatism, Melancholic Hope, and Redemptive Hope

IN THIS BOOK, I have used a set of predictions made by the American philosopher Richard Rorty—a set of predictions made in 1997 and 1998 about the twenty-first century—to consider why the academic Left might be blamed for the current state of American politics. In so doing, I traced the neglect of the poor by the academic Left back to its Cold War roots—namely academic McCarthyism—and demonstrated that fear of losing one's job and scholarly status established the habit within the academy of severely lessening the degree to which we remember and teach about the unemployed and the working poor. If we are indeed in the "dark years"—which is what Rorty predicts about this current time (2014–2044)—then the blame can be laid at the feet of the academy because we gave up on teaching and thinking about poverty. The unemployed and working poor are the ones who played a primary role in electing a "strongman" in the 2016 presidential election, and this "strongman" serves as one sign (among others) of Rorty's predictions concerning the "dark years" coming true.

Also, I explained and examined Rorty's predictions about American social life after the "dark years." These years represent Rorty's vision for social hope. I critiqued Rorty's vision on two fronts. First, his political philosophy maintains and repeats the residue of neoliberalism. A return to the neoliberalism of 1980–2007 (the time of Rorty's death) or 1980–2013 (Rorty's prediction) does not offer a legitimate, substantive view of what deserves our hope.

Second, his philosophy of religion—which predicts and states that Pauline charity will become the "only law"—ought to be judged as unrealistic precisely because those who claim to give Paul the most authority in their beliefs and in their lives seem to be the furthest from practicing Pauline charity. I refer here to American Evangelical Christians, and I demonstrated in chapter 7 how—in addition to the academic Left—American Evangelical Christians are responsible for the current "dark years" in this country. Far from practicing a social gospel—which Rorty claims fits in within his secular vision for social hope—American Evangelical Christians practice faith without charity.

In chapter 6, I gave an analysis of what it means for a philosopher to make predictions. This analysis led to a better understanding of the business of making predictions, and it also problematized Rorty's predictions on the terms of his own philosophical insights. His predictions fall in line either with Enlightenment views of digression and progression (my view) or with the overly religious tendency to predict a time of tribulation—the "dark years"—before a time of bliss and flourishing. Either way, Rorty puts himself in a tradition of thought that he actively refused throughout his writing career.[1]

There are two other problems with Rorty's predictions—both of which guide the conclusion to this book. First, Rorty's object of hope remains American politics. Second, Rorty's predictions of the "dark years" betray and negate his own self-description as the philosopher of hope within the American philosophical tradition. The remainder of this conclusion, therefore, will provide a defense and explanation of these two lines of critique of Rorty's philosophy of hope and the nature of his predictions. In order to achieve this, I garner as much support as possible from other scholars who have written on Rorty's philosophy of hope.

For the first critique—that Rorty mistakenly makes American politics the proper, and perhaps only, object of hope within social life—I enlist Akiba Lerner's case for redemptive hope and Joseph Winters's description of melancholic hope. For the second critique—that Rorty's set of predictions negate or violate his self-description as a philosopher of hope—I engage with Robert Talisse's argument that Rorty's political philosophy, itself (even without the predictions), leads to a "hopeless politics."[2] Furthermore, Talisse's new book—*Overdoing Democracy*—allows me to tie the two critiques together and suggest that these "dark years" will come to an end when we

---

1. See Rorty, "Enlightenment and 'Postmodernism,'" ch. 2; see Rorty, "The Professor and the Prophet."

2. See Talisse, PCRR, 611–26.

turn our hopes away from American politics and toward more substantial relationships with one another.

MELANCHOLIC HOPE AND REDEMPTIVE HOPE

I find myself persuaded in two seemingly contradictory or opposite directions concerning the versions of hope that seem possible in relation to Rorty's political philosophy. On the one hand, the part of me who is a scholar of Jewish philosophy grasps onto Akiba Lerner's argument that Rorty's philosophy of hope works if and only if we supplement it with the theology of redemption found in Martin Buber's defense and explanation of the "I-Thou" relationship. On the other hand, the part of me who buys into Sigmund Freud's account of human nature deeply and painfully agrees with Joseph Winters's critique of Rorty's philosophy of hope on the grounds that it (a) fails to take seriously the problem of racism in the US and (b) refuses to consider the psychological impact of America's sins. Winters calls his version of hope melancholic hope. Which order to go in: Martin Buber or Sigmund Freud, melancholy or redemption, the promises of religion or the reality of racism?

Redemptive Hope

I begin with Akiba Lerner's account of redemptive hope because, rhetorically, melancholic hope provides a better lead into the next section on Rorty's "hopeless politics." Akiba Lerner is associate professor of Religious Studies at Santa Clara University and writes on the intersections between American philosophy and Jewish theology. Lerner attempts to marry Rorty's social hope with a Buber-inspired redemptive hope. Lerner does not critique Rorty's version of social hope but, rather, supplements it with the theology of redemption found in Buber's "I-Thou" relationship.[3] How does Buber's "I-Thou" relationship relate to Rorty's vision of social hope?[4]

First, Buber's "I-Thou" relationship establishes forms of trust that seem lacking within Rorty's vision of social hope. This trust results from the dialogical aspect of the "I-Thou" relationship, and it relates to hope in terms of our present and future relationships. According to Lerner, "We enter into dialogue with the hope for encounter and understanding, while simultaneously, we have the potential to come away with hope for future encounters."[5] This connection between hope and trust supplements—perhaps I should say thickens (in the sense that Michael Walzer uses the term[6])—Rorty's notion of solidarity because "the genuine solidarity that forms the basis of relationships and community" requires a substantial amount of trust.[7] This kind of trust takes effort, time, and work in *communal* relationships; therefore, it calls for more than reading novels in one's private life in order to shape one's imagination in relation to solidarity.[8]

Second, Buber's "I-Thou" relationship celebrates subjectivity—what Rorty considers one's private self—but connects subjectivity with responsibility. Lerner claims, in fact, that "one's responsibility for the other [is] the *basis* for subjectivity."[9] This means that the bourgeois liberal aspect of Rorty's vision for social hope falls short because Rorty argues for a limited understanding of our responsibility toward the other.[10]

3. Lerner prefers the word "complements" over "supplements": "The phenomenology of hope I perceive in Buber's work complements Rorty's postmetaphysical ideal of solidarity by providing an account for reimagining intersubjective encounters as an alternative foundation for solidarity and social hope" (Lerner, *RH*, 17); "Buber's exploration of the libidinal, spiritual, and existential dimensions that bind intersubjective encounters with the messianic ultimately complement Rorty's concept of social hope" (Lerner, *RH*, 20). In my judgment, however, Lerner's argument demonstrates that Buber's theology of redemption does more than complement Rorty's neo-pragmatism—hence my use of the verb "supplements" to describe Lerner's argument.

4. The argument of this section follows up on insights found in chapter 3 of Goodson, *SM*.

5. Lerner, *RH*, 54.

6. See Walzer's *Thick and Thin*.

7. Lerner, *RH*, 55.

8. Significantly, Rorty's former student Robert Brandom recently published a massive volume on trust: see Brandom's *A Spirit of Trust* (2019). In over eight hundred pages of arguments, however, Brandom never mentions the work of his teacher.

9. Lerner, *RH*, 56; emphasis added.

10. For more on my take on the relationship between subjectivity and responsibility, see Goodson, *SM*, ch. 3.

Third, Buber's "I-Thou" relationship borrows from the existentialist emphasis on *presence*. Although he admires the work of Martin Heidegger, Rorty does not seem to rely on this existentialist emphasis on *presence*—perhaps because he thinks it relies on making too hard of a distinction between presentation and representation.[11] For Buber, however, redemption becomes the name for a particular kind of presence that God has with humanity and that individuals might have with one another. Lerner writes,

> The grounding of redemptive hope in intersubjective encounters . . . follows from Buber's controversial interpretation of revelation as a moment of presence . . . . Revelation is not about specific legislation handed down . . . but rather lies in the *event* of presence as the *self* opens to *otherness*. God's revelation to humanity is . . . more about understanding oneself as existing in dialogic partnership with the process of completing the work of creation . . . . The sense of presence generated in revelation is renewed through the hope created by each moment of recognition.[12]

For Rorty, neither God's law nor God's presence should have any impact on our social hopes. For Buber, however, without God's presence we always remain at risk of treating other people as "its"—of objectifying them. This is what happens within neoliberalism: citizens are turned into either consumers or entrepreneurs or both. In my judgment, Rorty's political philosophy offers no out for treating others—both neighbors and strangers—as "its."

Does this third point suggests that Rorty's account of social hope requires what might be called a metaphysics of presence—which means that Buber's theology of redemption does not supplement Rorty's neo-pragmatism but, instead, replaces it? Akiba Lerner pushes back against affirming this question. In his chapter entitled, "Richard Rorty's Social Hope and Postmetaphysical Redemption," he argues that even Rorty's secular vision for social hope can handle Buber's version of redemption. According to Lerner, "Rorty's . . . appeal to separating the secular from the religious . . . was less relevant to his overall vision of social hope based on reconciling notions of contingency to solidarity."[13] When this separation comes into play, within Rorty's vision, it concerns more what the *reasons* for hopefulness

---

11. See Part 1 of Rorty's *Essays on Heidegger and Others*, 9–83.

12 Lerner, *RH*, 63.

13. Lerner, *RH*, 111.

are: "For Rorty . . . , social hope replaces fears for rewards and punishment in the next life."[14] Buber's theology of redemption also seeks to replace the "rewards and punishment" interpretation of the significance of following or failing to follow God's law, and his replacement concerns his theology of redemption centered around how the presence of God positively impacts our relationship with other people. This positive impact leads to redemptive hope. Because of this, Lerner makes the judgment, "Rorty's claim that becoming open to the narratives of other people's experiences and pain is . . . itself a redemptive performance of opening toward creating new descriptions for turning an *other* into *one of us*."[15] This "redemptive performance" is what Lerner labels as Rorty's postmetaphysical account of redemption, which provides a secular vision of social hope that has the ability to work alongside Martin Buber's theological version of redemptive hope.

In my judgment, Buber's theological version of redemptive hope adds to Rorty's vision of social hope an argument concerning why human beings need something beyond or higher—not necessarily in an old-school metaphysical sense—politics and political relationships for hopefulness. Although I admire Lerner's defense of Rorty's secular vision for "social hope" on the terms of Buber's "I-Thou" theology, my own interpretation of Rorty's vision is that he offers no way to keep politics accountable to higher standards. Obviously, Rorty leaves no room for politics to be held accountable to divine judgment. Furthermore, in his critique of Immanuel Kant's Enlightenment philosophy, he also leaves no room for politics to be held accountable to any type of moral judgment. In this regard, Rorty allows for politics to be our only object of hope. Granted, Rorty seeks a politics that achieves solidarity; however, his political philosophy remains too close to the politics of neoliberalism for it to be considered a legitimate hope for American citizens. Rorty does not envision "I-Thou" relationships among human beings; rather, the furthest he gets us is that we might treat both neighbors and strangers better because doing so will enhance aesthetic opportunities within our own private lives.[16]

For those readers who are religious believers, my argument entails that Buber's "I-Thou" relationship can become the object of our hope for our interpersonal relationships. For those readers who are nonreligious believers,

14. Lerner, *RH*, 97.

15. Lerner, *RH*, 95.

16 Even Rorty's explicit argument for redemption, in "Redemption from Egotism," only gets us this far.

we can set our hopes on a strong moral sense of our interpersonal relationships. We are not limited by the tenets of neoliberalism, where other people are always instrumentalized for economic purposes; we are not limited by a politics that only allows for others to be either neighbors or strangers under the name of secular solidarity. Rather, we can develop "I-thou" relationships that are best understood as in-depth, substantial friendships—friendships neither controlled by nor determined by the politics of neoliberalism. Rorty's vision for social hope fails to get us to these in-depth, substantial friendships.

Melancholic Hope

Joseph R. Winters is assistant professor of Religious Studies at Duke University. Reading his *Hope Draped in Black: Race, Melancholy, and the Agony of Progress* offers a transformative experience, especially for white Americans. I would go as far as to say that Winters's book proves Rorty wrong when he claims, in "Redemption from Egotism," that argumentative books will not be what transforms readers in the shift out of the "dark years." In *Hope Draped in Black*, Winters offers a strong critique of Rorty's *Achieving Our Country* and constructs an account of what he calls melancholic hope that borrows from the work of Sigmund Freud.

More precisely, Winters builds from Judith Butler's adoption and explanation of Sigmund Freud's argument in "Mourning and Melancholia."[17] Winters emphasizes how Freud's description of melancholia can be understood as a kind of hope—which he calls melancholic hope. Winters begins by claiming that Freud thinks of "the work of mourning" as "a sign of hope" but argues "a different kind of hope is opened up when we confront the intractability of loss or the ways various forms of unrecognized loss both shape and puncture our social worlds and relationships."[18] This "different kind of hope" comes to be described by Winters as "melancholic hope."[19] Melancholic hope, therefore, provides a name for the type of hope involved with the confrontation of "the intractability of loss or the ways various forms of unrecognized loss . . . shape and puncture our . . . relationships."[20]

17. See Butler, *Precarious Life*, 20–21; see Freud, "Mourning and Melancholia," 201–18.

18. Winters, *HDB*, 19.

19. Winters, *HDB*, 248–51.

20. Winters, *HDB*, 19.

Instead of equating melancholia with hopelessness, Winters finds a non-deceitful account of hope when understood in terms of melancholia. He writes that melancholia "becomes an occasion to be unsettled and opened up by painful, fragmented accounts of [broken relationships]. This melancholic attachment to . . . loss . . . makes possible a different kind of future than the one imagined by the proponents of progress."[21] Although he thinks of it on a macro scale, Winters's critique of the notion of progress also applies to the micro scale of personal relationships in the sense that thinking in terms of individual progression risks becoming self-deceived in terms of self-improvement and self-righteousness. We can be hopeful and still be reconciled with our losses rather than think that we progress past those losses in some way. In fact, to be hopeful without self-deceit means that we reconcile ourselves to the brokenness and loss experienced in life without making the further judgment that we progress past them in a way where they no longer impact us as persons. Winters gives us three verbs for outlining the tenets of melancholic hope: *"melancholic hope exposes . . . , melancholic hope cultivates . . .* , and *melancholic hope imagines."*[22]

In his chapter entitled "Figures of the Postracial," Winters strongly critiques the relationship between hope and pride in Rorty's *Achieving Our Country*. Winters couches his critique of Rorty in the Freudian terms of melancholy:

> Rorty argues . . . that there has been too much melancholy in the intellectual Left since the 1960s, a trend that prevents . . . intellectuals from expressing pride in the nation's achievements, from hoping and struggling for a better America and world . . . . [H]e suggests that the possibility of change depends on balancing hope and melancholy, or in his terms, pride and shame.[23]

Five pages later, Winters claims: "Pride and hope, according to Rorty, must outweigh shame and melancholy if we are to continue and advance these struggles."[24]

Rorty begins *Achieving Our Country* with the well-crafted sentence, "National pride is to countries what self-respect is to individuals: a necessary condition for self-improvement."[25] Too much of it (national pride),

21. Winters, *HDB*, 19.

22. Winters, *HDB*, 248; emphasis added.

23. Winters, *HDB*, 207.

24. Winters, *HDB*, 212.

25. Rorty, *AOC*, 3.

Rorty reasons, produces "bellicosity and imperialism," yet not enough of it (national pride) "makes energetic and effective debate about national policy unlikely."[26] With this argument, Rorty applies a golden mean approach to the question of patriotism: excessive patriotism means "bellicosity and imperialism," and I would add unhealthy nationalism; a total lack of patriotism, which Rorty claims has become a characteristic of the academic Left, becomes analogous to a lack of self-respect.

Why has the academic Left become unpatriotic?[27] The academic Left has prioritized a sense of shame concerning American history and society over that of patriotism and pride in country. For Rorty, this shame takes the Left in the wrong direction. Winters describes Rorty's thinking on the matter in this way:

> Even as Rorty acknowledges the play between pride and shame, he ultimately suggests that the former emotion must outweigh the latter. If this is the case, one might wonder what "productive" work memory and shame do besides chasten national pride and prevent pride from becoming imperialistic. His insistence on pride's outweighing shame suggests that hope for a better future and nation must outweigh and ultimately resolve the dissonant effects of melancholy, of cultivating a heightened sensitivity to historical loss, suffering, and cruelty.[28]

For Rorty, shame is counterproductive in relation to hope and pride. In *Achieving Our Country*, shame becomes a problematic category—especially within the academic Left. In *Philosophy and Social Hope*—published a year after *Achieving Our Country*—Rorty claims that shame will lead to sympathy. In *Philosophy and Social Hope*, the ones who feel shame are not the academic Left but those citizens who have helped to bring about the "dark years" because their shame has led to fear and hatred. We overcome the "dark years" when the same shame turns into sympathy instead of fear and hatred. The difference seems to be that the academic Left finds the externals of American history shameful while the citizens whose shame leads them to fear and hatred locate shame internally in themselves. If this interpretation of Rorty is correct, and I believe that it is (and see no real alternative),

---

26. Rorty, *AOC*, 3.

27. My answer to this question follows the direction of Joseph Winters. For Rorty's full answer, see his essay "The Unpatriotic Academy," in *PSH*, 252–54.

28. Winters, *HDB*, 208–9.

then Rorty's different accounts of shame ought to be judged as problematically patronizing toward those not part of the academic Left.

This priority of pride over shame relates to Rorty's version of hope within *Achieving Our Country*. In Winters's words, "Hope, [Rorty] suggests, requires a strong identification with one's country, its ideals, achievements, and losses."[29] To the same extent that shame prevents national pride, shame also thwarts hope. For Rorty, hope relates to the achievements, ideals, *and* losses of one's country.

Winters, however, says Rorty's understanding of "losses" falls short when it comes to telling the full truth about the sins of racism in the US. For Winters, we need a version of hope that not only allows for those losses but, in fact, employs shame as part of hope—without a dichotomous relationship between the two. Winters claims that we need

> a world in which hope is not divorced from shame and melancholy but enabled by these affects and dispositions; in fact, hope would involve the capacity to be figuratively wounded, undone, and transformed by the violence and suffering that selves are always implicated in, particularly the violence that sustains racial and national formations. In opposition to notions of hope that rely on fortifying and reinforcing established identities, an alternative hope might link the possibility of a better world to cultivating practices and interactions marked by receptivity, vulnerability, and heightened attunement to loss and damage. This would be a risky, precarious hope prompted by desires to build new relationships and communities, modes of coexistence that are suspicious of narratives that transform trauma into an instance of progress or national pride.[30]

I fully agree with Winters concerning how we need to bring a sense of shame together with hope, and Rorty's version of social hope does not get us there. In both of his accounts of shame—found in *Achieving Our Country* and in *Philosophy and Social Hope*—shame either has to be overcome (*AOC*) or it serves as a means to sympathy (*PSH*).[31] Such a transformation will happen magically.

---

29. Winters, *HDB*, 208.

30. Winters, *HDB*, 212–13.

31. When I defined hope as the "realistic, reasonable, and virtuous use of one's imagination" in *Strength of Mind*, I can add to that now the claim that shame aids us in attending to the "realistic" part of my definition (see Goodson, *SM*, ch. 8).

His phrase for this kind of hope, this alternative to Rorty's brand of hope, is melancholic hope—which "acknowledges inescapable tensions and conflicts when it comes to recognition, remembrance, and the legacy of racial difference."[32] Winters argues for "a hope draped in black, a hope made possible by melancholy, remembrance, and the contemplation of suffering and loss," and he seeks a hope "more promising than progress and its cognates for thinking about and reimagining black people's diverse strivings and the modern legacy of race more broadly."[33] According to Winters, possibilities "open up when we think hope and melancholy together, when vulnerability to the suffering of others becomes a site for a different kind of future and imaginary."[34] Winters's use of the word imaginary echoes my own definition of hope as the "realistic, reasonable, and virtuous use of one's *imagination*."

We should be melancholic about the classist, racist, and sexist past of the US while simultaneously remain hopeful about its future. Indeed, this is what James Baldwin means when he uses the phrase "achieving our country."[35] Rorty's *Achieving Our Country* is not written with this realization and sense of melancholy required for "achieving our country."

RORTY'S FAILURES AS A PHILOSOPHER OF HOPE AND A PRAGMATIST

In *Introducing Prophetic Pragmatism*, Brad Elliott Stone dares me to challenge labeling Rorty as a "pragmatist." The context of the dare is that, in *Introducing Prophetic Pragmatism*, I spend a whole chapter wondering aloud whether "pragmatist" serves as the best label for Cornel West's thinking. Stone says that I would never wonder aloud about labeling William James or Richard Rorty a pragmatist.[36]

So here we are: I spend the remainder of this conclusion challenging the label of pragmatist as it applies to Rorty's thinking. I think that the problem of Rorty's set of predictions can be stated in a two-fold way. First, Rorty misapplies the logic of pragmatism in those texts where he makes predictions: *Achieving Our Country, Philosophy of Social Hope* ("Looking

---

32. Winters, *HDB*, 249.

33. Winters, *HDB*, 243.

34. Winters, *HDB*, 243.

35. More on this phrase later in the "Conclusion."

36. See Goodson and Stone, *Introducing Prophetic Pragmatism*, ch. 3.

Backwards from 2095"), and "Atheism and Anti-clericalism" (in *The Future of Religion*). Second, Rorty's predictions do not represent what a philosopher of hope ought to argue. In his essay "A Pragmatist Critique of Richard Rorty's Hopeless Politics," Robert Talisse aims to prove—totally independent of Rorty's predictions (Talisse does not address Rorty's set of predictions)—that Rorty's political philosophy as a whole ought to be judged as a failure on the terms of a philosophy of hope and on the terms of pragmatism. I apply Talisse's argument to Rorty's set of predictions.

Robert Talisse is the W. Alton Jones Professor of Philosophy at Vanderbilt University, and he writes mostly on political philosophy and pragmatism.[37] In this section, I build upon and engage with Talisse's 2001 essay: "A Pragmatist Critique of Richard Rorty's Hopeless Politics." In the next section, I engage with Talisse's 2019 publication: *Overdoing Democracy: Why We Must Put Politics in Its Place*. Borrowing from Talisse's critiques of Rorty, my final judgment on Rorty's set of predictions is *they fail his readers on the terms of both hope and pragmatism*.

In "A Pragmatist Critique of Richard Rorty's Hopeless Politics," Talisse defends the thesis: "Rorty's antifoundationalist politics is insufficient to address social realities and moreover unable to foster the kind of pragmatic social hope he seeks to inspire. Hence Rorty's political vision is quite . . . hopeless."[38] Talisse attempts to translate Rorty's political philosophy down to two premises and a conclusion:

a. One cannot achieve a proof of democracy of the sort the foundationalist wants.

b. Once the foundationalist project is abandoned, all that is left for political philosophy is the antifoundationalist enterprise of offering idealizations of current practices.

c. Democracy is best served by antifoundationalism.[39]

Based on these premises, which seem to accurately portray how Rorty reasons about democracy and politics, Talisse makes "a pragmatist rejoinder to Rorty": "So I grant (a) in the list of Rorty's commitments. What pragmatists

---

37. Usually, readers find his publications with an additional name attached: Scott Aikin, another philosophy professor at Vanderbilt. In what I am engaging with in this conclusion, however, Talisse is the single author.

38. Talisse, PCRR, 612.

39. Talisse, PCRR, 615.

such as myself do not grant is (b), and a fortiori we do not grant (c)."[40] Why can pragmatists not grant (b) and, therefore, (c) as well?

Because, Talisse says, "Rorty's 'foundationalism or antifoundationalism' is a false dichotomy, and I do not think that the purposes of democracy will be best served by an antifoundationalist vocabulary and self-image."[41] The fallacy of false dichotomy committed by Rorty leads to significant problems with Rorty's political philosophy.[42] Talisse makes the judgment, for instance, that "it is unclear how Rorty can make the distinction between 'real' democracy and tyranny disguised as democracy while remaining faithful to his antifoundationalism."[43] In this way, the pragmatist problem with Rorty's political philosophy is not the fallacy itself but the consequences of the fallacy. In the end, "Rorty's view is insufficient to deal with certain political realities that threaten contemporary democracy . . . , [and] it is unable to inspire the kind of social hope that Rorty takes to be the principal objective of political theory."[44]

The example used by Talisse for how Rorty's political philosophy fails "to deal with certain political realities that threaten contemporary democracy" involves racism and white supremacy. Talisse writes,

> Members of white supremacist or other racist organizations certainly promote a certain vision of the "utopian future of our community" [Rorty's phrase], a particular image of what is best in our culture. We cannot treat racists as "mad" [Rorty's word for racists] *and* maintain that "limits of sanity" are set by the contingencies of community, for, in this case, the "madmen" are *members* of my community . . . . Rorty must either introduce some ad hoc qualifications to the terms "ethnocentrism," "idealization," and "social practice," such that racists will necessarily not count as "one of us," or he will have to concede that the modern democratic state is home to persons who promote views that differ substantially from his own.[45]

---

40. Talisse, PCRR, 619.

41. Talisse, PCRR, 619.

42. Readers ought to note that I demonstrated above how Rorty commits the fallacy of false dichotomy in his philosophy of religion; Talisse demonstrates how he commits the same fallacy in his political philosophy.

43. Talisse, PCRR, 621.

44. Talisse, PCRR, 621.

45. Talisse, PCRR, 622.

Applying Talisse's reasoning to Rorty's set of predictions: Rorty's political philosophy has no way to safeguard against the rise of racism and white supremacy predicted by Rorty in what he labels the "dark years."

Adding onto Talisse's critique, at the heart of pragmatism remains a commitment to the relationship between goodness and truth.[46] Rorty disregards this relationship in his political philosophy, which means that his political philosophy should not be labeled as pragmatist. Rorty considers William James a fellow antifoundationalist, so I am not making a foundationalist critique of Rorty's political philosophy. Like Talisse, I am making a pragmatist critique of Rorty's political philosophy. In *Pragmatism*, James claims, "[T]ruth is one species of good, and not . . . a category distinct from good. . ."—by which, he means, "*The true is the name of whatever proves itself to be good in the way of belief, and good, too, for definite assignable reasons.*"[47] Throughout his career, Rorty explicitly disregards "truth."[48] In his set of predictions, we witness Rorty failing on the terms of pragmatism because his predictions are not "good in the way of belief."[49]

Evidence for my Jamesean critique of Rorty comes from a former student in my Fall 2016 course, PHIL 255: American Philosophy.[50] In her final research paper for that course, Heather Gilmore wrote in December 2016—a month after Trump's election:

> If I am completely honest, I feel a bit cheated. As a young adult new to political influence, it seems to me that there was nothing that I could have done to prevent Trump's election and all that means for educated citizens. Reading Rorty's ideas on the cultural Left gave me hope but then, because of current events, reading his prediction led me to despair. All I can do is hope the first part of his prediction is a coincidence and the second part hyperbole. I am holding on to the fact that, most likely, there are factors that will fully prevent too much damage being done—damage that relates to the ways in which his prediction so far seems to be actualized. Perhaps our hope is that other people see his prediction come true, which will be enough to encourage individuals to work to prevent the rest of it from coming true. Perhaps the knowledge

46. See James, *Pragmatism*, 17–32, 76–91.

47. James, *Pragmatism*, 30; emphasis in original.

48. See Long, "Richard Rorty and Methodological Nominalism."

49. James, *Pragmatism*, 30.

50. The timing of the course, Fall 2016, is significant in relation to the subject matter of the present book.

of our regression will call to action the cultural Left and everyone who has a moral compass. We can make strides to prevent the forthcoming of Rorty's predicted Dark Years.[51]

Gilmore's reflections allow us to make two inferences. First, Rorty's predictions are not good, because they do not lead his readers to goodness but to an unhealthy despair. Pragmatists argue and teach us that arguments, ideas, and theories become valuable only to the extent that they inspire their readers toward action, improved practices, and practical reasoning. Rorty's predictions fail on this pragmatist account.

Second, to the extent that there is any, the goodness of Rorty's predictions can be found only by *reconnecting goodness and truth*. This reconnection means that we treat Rorty's set of predictions against his antifoundationalist political philosophy. On Gilmore's terms, the best that Rorty's predictions can do seems to be that they might invite us to reason together about the following: if "his prediction come *true*," then that "will be enough to encourage individuals to work to prevent the rest of it [his other predictions] from coming true" and "the knowledge of our regression will call to action ... everyone who has a moral compass."

Gilmore's reflections also leads us back to Talisse's second indictment against Rorty: Rorty's political philosophy "is unable to inspire the kind of social hope that Rorty takes to be the principal objective of political theory."[52] Concerning this indictment, Talisse really piles on Rorty's antifoundationalism:

> Rorty's political antifoundationalism places liberal democracy on a philosophical par with tyranny. There is, Rorty insists, nothing one can say against tyranny that should count as a good reason for the tyrant to become a democrat.... Once political theorists give up the "distraction" of trying to develop foundations for democracy, they can take up their proper work of helping to inspire within democratic citizens the social hope requisite to "achieving" our country.... [Yet,] an essential component of hope is the confidence that what is hoped for is in some relevant way *worth* achieving and *better* than the other things that might develop. Yet Rorty's antifoundationalism does not allow one to maintain that democracy is in any relevant way *better* than ... tyranny. Hence Rorty's "social hope" must [mean that] we must hope to achieve that which we no longer can think is *worth* achieving, we

51. Gilmore, "The Prediction," 8.
52. Talisse, PCRR, 621.

must draw inspiration from that which we contend is essentially not inspiring.[53]

Applying Talisse's reasoning to Rorty's set of predictions: Rorty's predictions about the "dark years" commit a similar mistake that Talisse identifies with the whole of Rorty's political philosophy. Rorty claims to defend a social hope, yet his way of reasoning leads to a different consequence than hopefulness. In the case of his predictions, however, the antifoundationalism is not the cause of the mistake; rather, the cause of the mistake concerns the regressive nature of Rorty's predictions: the "dark years" simply have to be lived through and tolerated, and there will be neither hope nor progress for thirty years. The philosopher of hope leads his readers to despair and hopelessness.

WHY POLITICS SHOULD NOT MONOPOLIZE OUR HOPES

In light of these critiques of Rorty's predictions, it might seem a reasonable conclusion to say that the *most hopeful response* to the "dark years" involves better politics. This is not my conclusion. My conclusion, instead, concerns why politics should no longer monopolize our hopes.

I blame neoliberalism, again, for inviting us to think that politics ought to be the best and highest object of our hope. Neoliberalism has fooled us into thinking that we should direct our hopes toward politics. It also follows from this that in no way does a return to the neoliberalism of the 1980s, 1990s, and 2000–2013 represent what we should hope for after the "dark years."

In *Overdoing Democracy: Why We Must Put Politics in Its Place*, Talisse argues that we have given too much authority over to politics in our everyday lives. There is "a dimension of democracy's trouble that has been overlooked," he claims, which "has to do with the *ubiquity* of democratic politics, the saturation of social life with activities and projects that are overtly organized around the categories and divisions of current politics— the political saturation of social space."[54] His examples of how this works are illuminating if not frustrating:

> [C]ommercial spaces have become more . . . politically homogeneous. As is commonly observed in popular media, Walmart and

53. Talisse, PCRR, 624.
54. Talisse, OD, 4.

Target serve politically distinct clientele, as do Dunkin' Donuts and Starbucks, as well as Chick-fil-A and Chipotle. Not incidentally, commercial marketing is now explicitly designed to target customers based on their political identities . . . . Starbucks overtly aims to appeal to the cosmopolitan self-image of the broadly liberal demographic it seeks to serve. Dunkin' Donuts strives to associate coffee and doughnuts with the patriotic value of hard work . . . , thereby aiming to capture conservative customers who want inexpensive caffeine and carbohydrates rather than the momentary semblance of being in a foreign country.[55]

We have very few social spaces that are not politicized. This monopoly enjoyed by American politics and the overuse of political identities renders it even more difficult to cultivate deep friendships, develop relationships with those who view the world differently, and establish connections with others outside of the roles of conservative or liberal. The monopoly enjoyed by politics makes life and relationships seem somewhat hopeless.

If we should not put our hopes in American politics, then what should become the object of hope? In order to answer this question, I remain with Talisse's *Overdoing Democracy*—which, in this case, helps me to clarify and identify two positions somewhere between which I seek to fall. Talisse narrates our object of hope in an either/or way:

> More and better politics cannot be the solution to the problem . . . because *politics is the problem*. If we hope to repair our democracy, we need to find occasions to do more than "reach across the aisle"; we need also to devise cooperative endeavors in which there is no aisle to reach across, activities where politics plays no part at all.[56]

In this passage, Talisse makes it clear that we currently find ourselves in a strong dichotomy; *either* politics remains our object of hope where solutions will be found, *or* we locate places that completely escape politics where those activities and relationships become the object of hope. Talisse does not employ a both/and logic for recognizing how both politics and non-politics might share in our object of hope.

I wish to locate a middle ground, when thinking about hope both within and beyond the "dark years," between the monopoly that American politics—and, particularly, neoliberalism—has on hope vs. Talisse's refusal of a both/and logic for thinking about hope. While I am quite sympathetic

---

55. Talisse, *OD*, 84; I removed italics in places where he uses them.

56. Talisse, *OD*, 7; italics in the original.

to Talisse's emphasis away from politics, it strikes me that a realistic version of hope—in terms of how I define hope as "the realistic, reasonable, and virtuous use of one's imagination"—must include aspects of both politics and non-politics. I suppose this means that the key word in this section heading is monopolize: politics should not *monopolize* our hopes, but politics can have a share of our hopes.

I believe that balancing melancholic hope with redemptive hope aids in locating this middle ground. In terms of melancholic hope, to the extent that hope remains hooked to American politics, our hope must be melancholic—in the Freudian sense—concerning both the past and present sins of American politics and society. We direct our melancholy toward the treatment of African Americans, Mexican Americans, Native Americans, the unemployed, and the working poor. Melancholic hope means that we remain truthful—which involves an element of shamefulness—concerning the sins of America while becoming hopeful about "achieving our country." A non-melancholic hope in American politics ought to be judged as an amnesic hope that refuses to tell the truth about who and what America has been and is.

I turn to the wisdom of James Baldwin in order to contrast the phrase "achieving our country" with that of "make America great again." There is no way to "make America great again," but we can achieve a country where "black and . . . white" realize that they "deeply need each other."[57] There is no way to "make America great again," but we can "really . . . become a nation—if we . . . achieve our identity, [achieve] our maturity."[58] There is no way to "make America great again," but "[i]f we . . . do not falter in our duty . . . , we may be able . . . to end the racial nightmare . . . , achieve our country, and change the history of the world."[59] If we achieve identity, maturity, and truthfulness about who and what we are, then we will achieve our country. If we remain nearsighted (about who and what we are), neglectful (of the truth), and nostalgic (for a problematic past), then we will fail to achieve the country that can be achieved. Baldwin's argument for "achieving our country" represents the extent to which we can direct our hopes in American politics.[60]

57. Baldwin, *FNT*, 97.

58. Baldwin, *FNT*, 97.

59. Baldwin, *FNT*, 105.

60. For further reflections on James Baldwin, from which I have learned a great deal, see Stout's *Democracy and Tradition*, 42–61.

In terms of redemptive hope, however, hope ought to be placed out-side of American politics. One object of hope outside of politics concerns our daily interactions and relationships. As a religious category, redemp-tion identifies the ways in which we might live with one another despite or through the brokenness that determines our relationships. Although this brokenness takes many forms, throughout this book I have identified neoliberalism as one of the ways in which relationships are broken and deceitful. I propose that we place our hopes in the redemption or repair (*tikkun olam*) of our everyday relationships. Our daily interactions and re-lationships might be over-determined by economics and politics, but they need not be.

I find that this notion of redemptive hope becomes a version of hope where Richard Rorty's work fails us in the twenty-first century. In the words of Áine Mahon:

> Specifically, [Rorty] reject[s] the significance of the ordinary . . . . "The Ordinary," Rorty writes, "strikes me as just the latest disguise of the *ontos on*," "an explanation of the obscure by the more ob-scure" . . . . In place of renewed attention to the disappointments and limitations of the everyday, Rorty counsels instead a complete changing of the subject, a happy transcendence of outmoded con-cern . . . . Rorty's rhetoric is one of liberation and release [from ordinary life].[61]

Redemptive hope gives us hope in our everyday relationships, and those relationships form our ordinary life. Rorty's version of social hope seeks to liberate or "release" us from ordinary life, not live more fully into it.[62] Rorty's version of social hope is neither hopeful nor useful (in the pragma-tist sense of the word). Again, we must conclude that Rorty's thinking fails on the terms of a philosopher of hope and as a pragmatist as well.

In conclusion, we need a melancholic hope when directing our hopes toward American politics. This seems necessary but not quite sufficient. We also need to direct our hope outside of American politics and into ac-tual, concrete relationships that we have in our ordinary lives. Redemptive hope serves as the best name for this kind of hope because it allows for both brokenness and repair in those relationships. Notice that both ver-sions of hope—melancholic hope and redemptive hope—require serious

61. Mahon, *The Ironist and the Romantic*, 33–34.

62. For my full account of ordinary life—and its difficulties, significance, and won-der—see Goodson, *SM*, ch. 5, 8.

and sobering truth-telling about both politics and personal relationships. Based upon Rorty's predictions, we have more brokenness and sinfulness to come—with no hope at all—for the next thirty years. According to Richard Rorty, these are the "dark years."

Appendix
Rorty's Regrets

CHAD KAUTZER AND EDUARDO Mendieta report that Richard Rorty gave a plenary address at a conference they hosted at Stony Brook.[1] Rorty's lecture is now published as its own chapter in Kautzer's and Mendieta's volume entitled *Pragmatism, Nation, and Race: Community in the Age of Empire* (2009). The conference took place in 2007, the same year as Rorty's death.

Rorty's contribution can be interpreted as a sign of regret. Regret about what? Although he never comes out and says it explicitly, I interpret his chapter as a sign of regret about his set of predictions that have been detailed in the present book. The title of his chapter becomes significant for my purposes: "The *Unpredictable* American Empire."[2]

In this appendix, I explain what I take to be Rorty's regrets about his own set of predictions.

RETURNING TO *ACHIEVING OUR COUNTRY*

Rorty tells his listening and reading audience that he wishes to return to a distinction he makes in *Achieving Our Country*: the academic Left vs. the Reformist Left. On the terms of the conference at Stony Brook,[3] the academic Left thinks of the United States as "a country that has always been imperial and hypocritical, one whose pretensions to moral worth have

---

1. See Kautzer and Mendieta, "Acknowledgements," in *Pragmatism, Nation, and Race*, xii.

2. See Rorty, "Unpredictable American Empire," 209–20; emphasis added.

3. See Kautzer and Mendieta, "Introduction: Community in an Age of Empire," in *Pragmatism, Nation, and Race*, 1–17.

always been undeserved," whereas the Reformist Left—the version of Left-ism defended by Rorty—sees the United States as a "republic that is always in danger . . . of becoming an empire" but maintains a "hopeful view of the United States."[4] He clarifies his own defense and view of the Reformist Left as those for whom "the image of America as lighting the way to freedom and justice might still be preserved."[5]

The problem with the academic Left, according to Rorty in 2007, still concerns class and race. Rorty puts it a bit differently, however, in 2007 than he did in 1997 and 1998. He says, "[W]e wanted the intellectuals to talk less about race and more about class, because we hoped that a political majority might be formed if poor white people and poor black people made common cause."[6] Instead of predicting this potential common cause, or the problems that come without such a common cause, Rorty claims that the best vision for Leftism now (2007) concerns *both* a love and pride in the USA *and* an unapologetic internationalism. However, he makes no predic-tions about how this comes to be in the twenty-first century.

Rorty chooses to reflect on the past rather than predict the future. Left-ists can love American politics and take pride in the American military for their willingness to remove evil dictators around the world, such as Sad-dam Hussein. In terms of internationalism, Leftists need to help individual nation-states remember how great they can be when they work together—as the allies did in WWII. He wishes that the United Nations could be more than it is, but both the European Union and the United States should neither wait nor yield to the United Nations for taking care of problematic actors on the international stage. He never allows himself to predict what will happen if/when the EU and US take such a lead on the international stage.

RORTY'S REGRETS?

In my explanation thus far, I have not given any evidence that Rorty regrets his previous predictions. I have established only that he does not repeat the task of making predictions. In the final paragraph of "The Unpredictable American Empire," however, I see signs of regret.

He gives himself an opportunity to reiterate his prediction about the 2016 presidential election. The "next three or four national elections," he

4. Rorty, "Unpredictable American Empire," 210–11.
5. Rorty, "Unpredictable American Empire," 213.
6. Rorty, "Unpredictable American Empire," 215.

says, will be very important for the future of the US Since this lecture is from 2007, he means the two elections that resulted in Barack Obama's eight years as POTUS; the 2016 election that resulted in Donald Trump's election; and the 2020 election. He does not reiterate his prediction from 1997—the one that went viral after Trump's election. Rather, he simply states:

> Whether America will have the necessary foresight and exercise the necessary prudence . . . will be determined, not by anything intrinsic to its nature or made inevitable by its history . . . but rather by a few million swing voters during the next three or four elections. That is one of the splendors, as well as one of the miseries, of a republic.[7]

In this passage, Rorty confirms a point I have made several times throughout the present book: he denies any type of determinism, both historical and natural determinism.

Rorty's final paragraph in this lecture given in 2007, however, goes against the set of predictions he made in 1997 and 1998. In his set of predictions, he knows the direction that the US goes: a direction containing neither foresight nor prudence but, rather, (fore)seeing the election of a "strongman" who takes us into the "dark years." In his set of predictions, he knows who to blame for the cause of this lack of foresight and imprudence: the academic Left. In this lecture from 2007, however, the academic Left is not blamed for the election of a "strongman" but described only as overly cynical and unpatriotic.

In this 2007 lecture, Rorty makes no claims about the future other than it remains open-ended in such a way that national elections deeply matter. I take this 180-degree turn in how he talks about the twenty-first century as a sign of regret that he predicted (a) the election of a "strongman," (b) the proliferation of gun violence, and (c) thirty years of darkness. Does this mean that the self-described philosopher of hope recognizes that his earlier set of predictions led to despair and hopelessness?

Rorty does not come across as any more hopeful in this 2007 lecture than he does in his set of predictions. He still regrets the direction(s) of the academic Left, and now he seemingly regrets predicting the "dark years" because of how much he loathes the academic Left. The object of Rorty's hope, in this 2007 lecture, remains American politics. Rorty's hope is only that we will leave the empire version of American politics behind and return to the republic version of American politics.

7. Rorty, "Unpredictable American Empire," 220.

Bibliography

Adams, John C. "Hope, Truth, and Rhetoric." In *Feminist Interpretations of Richard Rorty*, edited by Marianne Janack, 79–102. University Park, PA: Pennsylvania State University Press, 2010.

Alexander, Michelle. *The New Jim Crow: Mass Incarceration in the Age of Colorblindness*. New York: New Press, 2010.

Antaki, Mark. "The Turn to Imagination in Legal Theory: The Re-enchantment of the World?" *Law and Critique*, 23 (2012) 1–20.

Aristotle. *Poetics*. Translated by S. H. Butcher. http://classics.mit.edu/Aristotle/poetics.1.1.html.

Baert, Patrick. "Richard Rorty's Pragmatism and the Human Sciences." In *History of the Human Sciences* 15.1 (2001) 139–49.

Baldwin, James. *The Fire Next Time*. New York: Vintage, 1993.

Bernstein, Richard. "Richard Rorty: The Dark Years." *Public Seminar*, 2019. http://www.publicseminar.org/wp-content/uploads/2019/04/RortyTheDarkYears-Excerpt-1.pdf

———. "Rorty's Inspirational Liberalism." In *Richard Rorty*, edited by Charles Guignon and David R. Hiley, 124–38. New York: Cambridge University Press, 2003.

Bradbury, Ray. *Fahrenheit 451*. New York: Simon & Schuster, 2012.

Brandom, Robert. *A Spirit of Trust: A Reading of Hegel's Phenomenology*. Malden, MA: Belknap Press of Harvard University Press, 2019.

Brody, Sam. "The Grounds of Prophecy: Richard Rorty and the Hermeneutics of History." In *Rorty and the Prophetic: Jewish Engagements with a Secular Philosopher*, edited by Jacob L. Goodson and Brad Elliott Stone. Lanham, MD: Lexington Books, forthcoming.

Buckley, Christopher. *Thank You for Smoking*. New York: Random House, 1994.

Butler, Judith. *Precarious Life: The Powers and Mourning and Violence*. New York: Verso, 2004.

Cheever, Susan. *American Bloomsbury*. New York: Simon & Schuster, 2006.

Curtis, William M. *Defending Rorty: Pragmatism and Liberal Virtue*. New York: Cambridge University Press, 2015.

Dann, G. Elijah. *After Rorty: The Possibility of Ethics and Religious Belief*. New York: Continuum, 2006.

Dawisha, Karen. *Putin's Kleptocracy: Who Owns Russia?* New York: Simon & Schuster, 2015.

Dula, Peter. *Cavell, Companionship, and Christian Theology.* New York: Oxford University Press, 2010.

Edmundson, Mark. "Richard Rorty Is America's Most Controversial Philosopher." In *Wild Orchids and Trotsky: Messages from American Universities*, edited by Mark Edmundson, 30. New York: Penguin, 1993.

Emerson, Ralph Waldo. "The American Scholar." In *The Essential Writings of Ralph Waldo Emerson*, edited by Brooks Atkinson, 43–61. New York: Modern Library, 2000.

———. "Self-Reliance." In *The Essential Writings of Ralph Waldo Emerson*, edited by Brooks Atkinson, 132–52. New York: Modern Library.

Falcone, Michael. "Donald Trump Rode an Escalator to 2016 Presidential Announcement." *ABC News*, June 16, 2015. https://abcnews.go.com/Politics/donald-trump-rode-escalator-2016-presidential-announcement/story?id=31801433.

Foucault, Michel. *Courage to Truth.* Translated by Graham Burchell. New York: Picador, 2012.

Freud, Sigmund. *The Future of an Illusion.* Edited and translated by James Strachey. New York: W. W. Norton, 1961.

———. "Mourning and Melancholia." In *On Murder, Mourning, and Melancholia*, translated by Shaun Whiteside, 201–17. New York: Penguin, 2005.

Friedman, Megan. "A Book Written in 1998 Predicted Trump's Election Win in a Scary-Accurate Way: This Is So Eerie." *Cosmopolitan*, Nov. 21, 2016. https://www.cosmopolitan.com/politics/a8349320/richard-rorty-book-predicted-donald-trump-win/.

Gilmore, Heather. "The Prediction." Essay for Jacob Goodson's course PHIL 255: American Philosophy. Winfield, KS: Southwestern College, 2016.

Goodson, Jacob L. "'And the Greatest of These Is Love': Richard Rorty's Turn to Scripture." In *American Philosophers Read Scripture*, edited by Jacob L. Goodson. 193-203. Lanham, MD: Lexington Books, 2020.

———. "Left Behind? The New Testament and American Evangelical Christian Justification for War." In *Religion and Violence*, edited by Julia Snyder and Daniel Weiss. New York: Routledge, forthcoming.

———. "Pedagogical Hope and Practical Reasoning: Stanley Hauerwas and the Work of Philosophy." In *Journal of Scriptural Reasoning* 16.1 (2017). http://jsr.shanti.virginia.edu/back-issues/vol-16-no-1-november-2017-special-issue-honoring-the-work-of-stanley-hauerwas-and-his-friends/pedagogical-hope-and-practical-reasoning-stanley-hauerwas-and-the-work-of-philosophy/.

———. *Strength of Mind: Courage, Hope, Freedom, Knowledge.* Eugene, OR: Cascade, 2018.

Goodson, Jacob L., and Brad Elliott Stone. *Introducing Prophetic Pragmatism.* Lanham, MD: Lexington Books, 2019.

———, eds. *Rorty and the Religious: Christian Engagements with a Secular Philosopher.* Eugene, OR: Cascade, 2012.

Griggs, Mary Beth. "We've Been Predicting Eclipses for Over 2,000 Years. Here's How." *Popular Science Monthly*, Aug. 18, 2017. https://www.popsci.com/people-have-been-able-to-predict-eclipses-for-really-long-time-heres-how.

Gross, Neil. *Richard Rorty: The Making of an American Philosopher.* Chicago: University of Chicago Press, 2008.

Hauerwas, Stanley. *A Better Hope: Resources for a Church Confronting Capitalism, Democracy, and Postmodernity.* Grand Rapids: Brazos, 2000.

———. "Foreword." In *Rorty and the Religious: Christian Engagements with a Secular Philosopher,* edited by Jacob L. Goodson and Brad Elliott Stone, ix-x. Eugene, OR: Cascade, 2012.

———. "The Good Life." In *Minding the Web: Making Theological Connections,* 96–112. Eugene, OR: Cascade, 2018.

———. *Minding the Web: Making Theological Connections.* Eugene, OR: Cascade, 2018.

———. "Repent: The Kingdom Is Here." In *Christianity and the Social Crisis,* written by Walter Rauschenbusch, edited by Paul Rauschenbusch. New York: Harper Collins, 2007.

———. *The State of the University: Academic Knowledges and the Knowledge of God.* Malden, MA: Wiley-Blackwell, 2007.

———. *The Work of Theology.* Grand Rapids: Eerdmans, 2015.

Hauerwas, Stanley, and Jonathan Tran. "Sanctuary Politics: Being the Church in the Time of Trump." In *Minding the Web: Making Theological Connections,* 113–26. Eugene, OR: Cascade, 2018.

Heidegger, Martin. *Being and Time.* Translated by Joan Stambaugh. Albany, NY: State University of New York Press, 2010.

———. "'Only a God Can Save Us Now': An Interview with Martin Heidegger." Translated by David Schendler. *Graduate Faculty Philosophy Journal* 6.1 (1977) 5–27.

Heineman, Ben W., Jr. "The University in the McCarthy Era." *The Harvard Crimson,* June 17, 1965. https://www.thecrimson.com/article/1965/6/17/the-university-in-the-mccarthy-era/.

"In His Own Words: The President's Attacks on the Courts." *Brennan Center,* June 5, 2017. https://www.brennancenter.org/analysis/his-own-words-presidents-attacks-courts.

Jacoby, Susan. *The Age of American Unreason in a Culture of Lies.* New York, Vintage, 2018.

James, Henry. *The Ambassadors.* New York: Harper & Brothers, 1903.

James, William. *Pragmatism.* New York: Dover, 1995.

Johnson, Monte. "Stanley W. Moore Remembrance." *University of California, San Diego Philosophy Department: Institutional Memory,* edited by David Krogh, Apr. 29, 2010. https://ucsd-phil-dept-history.blogspot.com/2010/04/stanley-w-moore-remembrance.html.

Kant, Immanuel. "What Is Enlightenment?" In *Basic Writings of Kant,* edited by Allen W. Wood, 133–41. New York: Modern Library, 2001.

Kautzer, Chad, and Eduardo Mendieta, eds. *Pragmatism, Nation, and Race: Community in an Age of Empire.* Bloomington, IN: Indiana University Press, 2009.

Keen, Craig. *After Crucifixion: The Promise of Theology.* Eugene, OR: Cascade, 2013.

Kingsolver, Barbara. *The Poisonwood Bible.* New York: Harper, 1999.

Kotsko, Adam. *Neoliberalism's Demons: On the Political Theology of Late Capital.* Palo Alto, CA: Stanford University Press, 2018.

Kuipers, Ronald A. *Solidarity and the Stranger: Themes in the Social Philosophy of Richard Rorty.* Lanham, MD: University Press of America, 1997.

Latner, Steven. "'Populism' Is More Accurately 'Anti-elitism.'" *Financial Times,* Oct. 16, 2017. https://www.ft.com/content/4c14127c-b261-11e7-a398-73d59db9e399.

Lerner, Akiba. *Redemptive Hope: From the Age of Enlightenment to the Age of Obama.* New York: Fordham University Press, 2015.

Long, D. Stephen. "Richard Rorty and Methodological Nominalism." In *Rorty and the Religious: Christian Engagements with a Secular Philosopher*, edited by Jacob L. Goodson and Brad Elliott Stone, 23–45. Eugene, OR: Cascade, 2012.

Mahon, Áine. *The Ironist and the Romantic: Reading Richard Rorty and Stanley Cavell.* New York: Bloomsbury Academic, 2014.

Manne, Kate. *Down Girl: The Logic of Misogyny.* New York: Oxford University Press, 2019.

May, Todd. *Friendship in an Age of Economics: Resisting the Forces of Neoliberalism.* Lanham, MD: Lexington Books, 2014.

McCumber, John. *The Philosophy Scare: The Politics of Reason in the Early Cold War.* Chicago: University of Chicago Press, 2016.

————. *Time in the Ditch: American Philosophy and the McCarthy Era.* Evanston, IL: Northwestern University Press, 2001.

Melville, Herman. *Moby Dick.* New York: Harper & Brothers, 1851.

Metcalfe, Stephen. "Richard Rorty's Philosophical Argument for National Pride." *The New Yorker*, Jan. 10, 2017. https://www.newyorker.com/culture/cultural-comment/richard-rortys-philosophical-argument-for-national-pride.

Miller, Steven. *Community and Loyalty in American Philosophy.* New York: Routledge, 2018.

Nichols, David. *Ike and McCarthy: Dwight Eisenhower's Secret Campaign Against Joe McCarthy.* New York: Simon & Schuster, 2017.

Nietzsche, Friedrich. *The Gay Science.* Translated by Walter Kaufmann. New York: Vintage, 1974.

Nussbaum, Martha C. "Patriotism and Cosmopolitanism." In *The Cosmopolitanism Reader*, edited by Garrett W. Brown and David Held, 155–62. Malden, MA: Polity, 2010.

————. *Poetic Justice: The Literary Imagination and Public Life.* Boston: Beacon, 1997.

Peirce, C. S. "How to Make Our Ideas Clear." In *The Essential Peirce*, edited by Nathan Houser and Christian Kloesel, 1:124–40. Bloomington, IN: Indiana University Press, 1992.

Piston, Spencer. *Class Attitudes in America: Sympathy for the Poor, Resentment of the Rich, and Political Implications.* New York: Cambridge University Press, 2018.

Plato. *Apology.* Translated by Benjamin Jowett. http://classics.mit.edu/Plato/apology.html.

————. *The Republic.* Translated by Benjamin Jowett. http://classics.mit.edu/Plato/republic.html.

Popper, Karl. *The Open Society and Its Enemies.* Princeton, NJ: Princeton University Press, 2013.

————. "Prediction and Prophecy in the Social Sciences." In *Conjectures and Refutations: The Growth of Scientific Knowledge.* 2nd ed. New York: Routledge, 2002.

————. *The Poverty of Historicism.* 2nd ed. New York: Routledge, 2002.

Putnam, Hilary. *Words and Life.* Edited by James Conant. Cambridge, MA: Harvard University Press, 1994.

Quine, W. V. O., and Ullian, J. S. *The Web of Belief.* 2nd ed. New York: McGraw-Hill Education, 1978.

Rankin, Stephen. Review of *Strength of Mind: Courage, Hope, Freedom, Knowledge. Christian Higher Education* 18.4 (2019) 335–37.

Reno, R. R. "Nietzsche's Deeper Truth." *First Things*, Jan. 2008. https://www.firstthings.com/article/2008/01/nietzsches-deeper-truth.

Rescher, Nicholas. *Predicting the Future: An Introduction to the Theory of Forecasting*. Albany, NY: State University of New York Press, 1998.

Rorty, James. *Where Life Is Better: An Unsentimental American Journey*. New York: Andesite, 2015.

Rorty, James, and Moshe Decter. *McCarthy and the Communists*. Boston: Beacon, 1954.

Rorty, Richard. *Achieving Our Country: Leftist Thought in Twentieth-Century America*. Cambridge, MA: Harvard University Press, 1999.

———. *Against Bosses, Against Oligarchies*. Edited by Derek Nystrom and Kent Puckett. Charlottesville, VA: Prickly Pear, 1998.

———. "Anticlericalism and Atheism." In *The Future of Religion*, edited by Santiago Zabala, 29–41. New York: Columbia University Press, 2005.

———. *Contingency, Irony, and Solidarity*. New York: Cambridge University Press, 1989.

———. "The Continuity between the Enlightenment and 'Postmodernism.'" In *What's Left of Enlightenment?*, edited by Keith Michael Baker and Peter Hans Reill, 19–36. Palo Alto, CA: Stanford University Press, 2001.

———. *Essays on Heidegger and Others*. Philosophical Papers 2. New York: Cambridge University Press, 1991.

———. *An Ethics for Today: Finding Common Ground between Philosophy and Religion*. New York: Columbia University Press, 2010.

———. "Fraternity Reigns." *New York Time*, Sept. 29, 1996. https://www.nytimes.com/1996/09/29/magazine/fraternity-reigns.html.

———. *Philosophy and Social Hope*. New York: Penguin, 1998.

———. *Philosophy and the Mirror of Nature*. Princeton, New Jersey: Princeton University Press, 1979.

———. "Postmodernist Bourgeois Liberalism." In *Objectivity, Relativism, and Truth*, 197–202. Philosophical Papers 1. New York: Cambridge University Press, 1990.

———. "Pragmatism as Romantic Polytheism." In *Philosophy as Cultural Politics*. Philosophical Papers 4:27–40. New York: Cambridge University Press, 2007.

———. "The Professor and the Prophet." *Transition* 52 (1991) 70–78.

———. "Redemption from Egotism." In *The Rorty Reader*, edited by Christopher J. Voparil and Richard J. Bernstein, 389–405. Malden, MA: Wiley-Blackwell, 2010.

———. "Response to Jeff Stout." In *The Philosophy of Richard Rorty*, edited by Randall E. Auxier, 546–49. Chicago: Open Court, 2010.

———. "Trotsky and the Wild Orchids." In *Wild Orchids and Trotsky: Messages from American Universities*, edited by Mark Edmundson, 31–50. New York: Penguin, 1993.

———. "The Unpredictable American Empire." In *Pragmatism, Nation, and Race: Community in an Age of Empire*, edited by Chad Kautzer and Eduardo Mendieta, 209–20. Bloomington, IN: Indiana University Press, 2009.

Rothleder, Diane. *The Work of Friendship: Rorty, His Critiques, and the Project of Solidarity*. Albany, NY: State University of New York Press, 1999.

Rottenberg, Elizabeth. *Inheriting the Future*. Palo Alto, CA: Stanford University Press, 2005.

Saarinen, Esa. "Kindness to Babies and Other Radical Ideas." In *From Pragmatist Philosophy to Cultural Politics*, edited by Alexander Gröschner et al., 145–64. New York: Bloomsbury, 2013.

Schneewind, J. B. "Rorty on Utopia and Moral Philosophy." In *The Philosophy of Richard Rorty*, edited by Randall E. Auxier, 479–505. Chicago: Open Court, 2010.

Seal, Andy. "Why Richard Rorty Was Not a Prophet." *Society for U.S. History*, Nov. 21, 2016. https://s-usih.org/2016/11/why-richard-rorty-was-not-a-prophet/

Sellars, Wilfred. *Science and Metaphysics: Variations on Kantian Themes*. Atascadero, CA: Ridgeview, 2017.

Senior, Jennifer. "Richard Rorty's 1998 Book Suggested 2016 Election Was Coming." *New York Times*, Nov. 21, 2016. https://www.nytimes.com/2016/11/21/books/richard-rortys-1998-book-suggested-election-2016-was-coming.html.

Shrecker, Ellen. *Many Are the Crimes: McCarthyism in America*. Princeton, NJ: Princeton University Press, 1998.

———. *No Ivory Tower: McCarthyism and the Universities*. New York: Oxford University Press, 1986.

———. "Political Tests for Professors: Academic Freedom During the McCarthy Years." In *The University Loyalty Oath: A 50th Anniversary Retrospective*. Berkeley: University of California, 1999. http://www.lib.berkeley.edu/uchistory/archives_exhibits/loyaltyoath/symposium/schrecker.html.

Smith, James K. A. "Secularity, Globalization, and the Re-enchantment of the World." In *After Modernity? Secularity, Globalization, and the Re-enchantment of the World*, 3–15. Waco: Baylor University Press, 2008.

Steger, Manfred B., and Ravi K. Roy. *Neoliberalism: A Very Short Introduction*. New York: Oxford University Press, 2010.

Steinbeck, John. *The Grapes of Wrath*. New York: Viking, 1939.

Stiegler, Bernard. *The Re-enchantment of the World: The Value of Spirit against Industrial Populism*. New York: Bloomsbury, 2014.

———. *States of Shock: Stupidity and Knowledge in the 21st Century*. Malden, MA: Polity, 2015.

Stone, Brad Elliott. "Can There be Hope without Prophecy?" In *Rorty and the Religious: Christian Engagements with a Secular Philosopher*, edited by Jacob L. Goodson and Brad Elliott Stone, 153–72. Eugene, OR: Cascade, 2012.

Stout, Jeffrey. *Democracy and Tradition*. Princeton, NJ: Princeton University Press, 2004.

———. "Religion within the Bounds of Justice Alone." Lecture at Institute for American Religious and Philosophical Thought Conference, Asheville, NC, June 2019.

Sullivan, Shannon. *Good White People: The Problem with Middle-Class White Anti-racism*. Albany, NY: State University of New York Press, 2014.

Talisse, Robert. *Overdoing Democracy: Why We Must Put Politics in Its Place*. New York: Oxford University Press, 2019.

———. "A Pragmatist Critique of Richard Rorty's Hopeless Politics." *Southern Journal of Philosophy*, 39.4 (2001) 611–26.

Taylor, Charles. *A Secular Age*. Malden, MA: Belknap Press of Harvard University Press, 2018.

Thoreau, Henry David. "On Civil Disobedience." In *Walden and Other Writings*, edited by Brooks Atkinson, 665–93. New York: Modern Library, 1992.

Walzer, Michael. *Thick and Thin: Moral Arguments at Home and Abroad*. Notre Dame, IN: University of Notre Dame Press, 1994.

West, Cornel. "Goodbye, American Neoliberalism. A New Era Is Here" *The Guardian*, Nov. 17, 2016. https://www.theguardian.com/commentisfree/2016/nov/17/american-neoliberalism-cornel-west-2016-election.

Winters, Joseph. *Hope Draped in Black: Race, Melancholy, and the Agony of Progress*. Durham, NC: Duke University Press, 2016.

Author Index

Subject Index

Printed in Great Britain
by Amazon